YOU HAVE IT IN YOU!

EMPOWERED TO DO THE IMPOSSIBLE

SHERYL BRADY

Howard Books
A Division of Simon & Schuster, Inc.
New York   Nashville   London   Toronto   Sydney   New Delhi

Howard Books
A Division of Simon & Schuster, Inc.
1230 Avenue of the Americas
New York, NY 10020

First Howard Books trade paperback edition July 2013

HOWARD and colophon are trademarks of Simon & Schuster, Inc.

For information about special discounts for bulk purchases,
please contact Simon & Schuster Special Sales at 1-866-506-1949
or business@simonandschuster.com.

The Simon & Schuster Speakers Bureau can bring authors
to your live event. For more information or to book an event,
contact the Simon & Schuster Speakers Bureau at 1-866-248-3049
or visit our website at www.simonspeakers.com.

Designed by Davina Mock-Maniscalco

Manufactured in the United States of America

1 3 5 7 9 10 8 6 4 2

Library of Congress Cataloging-in-Publication Data
Brady, Sheryl, 1960-
You have it in you : empowered to do the impossible / Sheryl Brady.
p. cm.
1. Self-actualization (Psychology)—Religious aspects—Christianity.
2. Success—Religious aspects—Christianity. 3. Christian Life.
4. Suffering—Religious aspects—Christianity. I. Title.
BV4598.2.B74 2012
248.4—dc23
2012013492

ISBN 978-1-4516-7410-1
ISBN 978-1-4516-8190-1 (pbk)
ISBN 978-1-4516-7412-5 (ebook)

I write these words in honor and celebration of the life and legacy of my father, Mr. Lee Warren. I'm not sure if I will ever know why I had to give you up *like* I did *when* I did. Fifty-two years young is just too early to say good-bye. What I am sure of is this: You dropped a mantle, I picked it up, and by the grace of God, and the fact that your voice has been added to the cloud of witnesses who are cheering me on from the balcony of heaven, I WILL finish "my/our" course with joy!

CONTENTS

Alice ✓

CONTENTS

FOREWORD

THERE ARE MANY THINGS THAT COULD BE SAID ABOUT the author of this book. She is a voice to the nations, a psalmist, a writer, a worshipper, a pastor, and a leader. When she stepped into an arena where women are often not met with the same welcome their male counterparts enjoy, she neither apologized for her femininity nor acquiesced to bitterness. Instead she calmly and humbly sought to serve her generation in whatever way she could. To be sure, her humble spirit and biblical prowess has earned her respect even amongst those who are skeptical of women in ministry.

I believe that she is unveiling yet more creativity and relevance every day. As she releases more and more of her intrinsic gift, I watch with amazement as she not only blossoms herself, but also helps others to unlock, unmask, and unearth the hidden treasure they were often oblivious to before encountering her ministry.

I met Pastor Sheryl Brady and her family roughly twenty years ago in Cleveland while ministering. Ultimately, her family moved to West Virginia and became a part of our congregation. Later, when I moved to Dallas, they joined us here and continued to serve under the newly formed church, The Potter's House, which opened in 1996.

Along with her husband, Bishop Joby Brady, she's traveled around the country ministering both as a psalmist and now as part of a fine ministry team between the two of them. Bishop Brady is a bulwark of ministerial expertise in his own right, yet there seems to be no rivalry. They exhibit a sense of completion in their union, not competition.

I have watched Sheryl Brady grow from a psalmist and worship leader into a scholar and spiritual technician of the word of God. Having observed her up close, I can attest that her integrity is impeccable and her ability to access the presence of God is earning her a growing reputation around the world. I was delighted to learn that she has decided to share her deep revelations and worship extracted from her own life as well as illustrations throughout Scripture that would help other people to live on purpose.

I have observed her as a daughter, wife, mother, member, and now pastor of The Potter's House of North Dallas. In each of these areas, she continues to produce a fruitful, purposeful, and meaningful life. It is my hope that you will start and continue on the journey that she has prescribed, and I feel confident that by the time you finish reading this book, you will discover the deep intrinsic treasure that God has placed inside of you. In so doing, you will unearth it and share it with your generation as generously as she has outlined in the pages before you.

If you believe, as I do, that when Paul declared in the book of Ephesians that the exceeding riches of His inheritance is hidden in His people, you will want those riches to be identified in your own life and to find your God-given talents and purpose. This is a GPS guide filled with Scriptural insights that will usher you into a richer, fuller expression of yourself on earth. I am sure that you will benefit from this read and be transformed beyond the dismal into the delightful, from the tranquil to the transformational, fulfilled individual you were created to be.

To those of you who have not met her, I am honored to be a forerunner to prepare your heart for the electrifying ministry of Pastor Sheryl Brady.

—Bishop T. D. Jakes

THE SIGNIFICANCE OF FEELING INSIGNIFICANT

Have you ever found yourself in a situation so unexpected, so unlike anything else in your life, that you had to ask, *How in the world did I get* here? Amid a flood of emotions, thoughts, and ideas, you suddenly realize that something—*everything*—has changed around you. Like a runner crossing the finish line at her first marathon, maybe you experienced the thrill of working hard and achieving something you've always wanted, overcoming the challenges that made the goal once feel impossible. Or maybe you experienced a loss so devastating that you fell to the ground, unsure if you could ever get back on your feet.

In both instances, time stands still, the landscape shifts, and we discover what's really inside us, way down deep at the core of our being. Not just what we say we believe, but what we truly believe about who we are, who God is, and what life is all about—what we're made of. In these moments, we may feel exhilarated, powerless, uncertain, afraid, inspired, defeated, energized, drained, or a combination of them all. Whether a wonderful opportunity or an agonizing trial, such situations make us all want to know, *Do I have what it takes to get through this?*

Whether you realize it or not, how you answer this question carries life-changing significance for you and for everyone around you. How you answer this question determines the actions you will take that will set the direction of your life's journey. How you answer this question either focuses your attention on your own limitations of self and circumstance, or it draws you to discover God's limitless power and bountiful provision within you.

While I'd like to believe it gets easier each time I come through these how-did-I-get-here moments, I find that the stakes just seem to get higher. I believe this is true for all of us. Just as we grow in our faith by experiencing God's faithfulness and goodness, just as we're feeling a bit more secure about who we are and what we can do, we're presented with new challenges, new mountains to climb, new trails to blaze. Recently I experienced one of these excursions into unknown territory—a life-changing invitation to discover more of what God has placed inside of me. It all began with a most unexpected late-night phone call.

MIDDLE-OF-THE-NIGHT PHONE CALLS RARELY BRING good news. So when I heard my cell's familiar ring from my nightstand, I reluctantly rolled over and fumbled for the phone. I kept reaching and reaching and couldn't find it in the usual spot. Finally my hand grasped the edge of the nightstand, but still no phone—only a couple of books falling to the floor. My phone kept ringing.

By now I was sitting up as my sleepy eyes adjusted to the darkness. The red digital glow of the clock revealed it was after 1 A.M. Still ringing, the phone was right there—exactly where it always was. I grabbed it and managed to say, "Hello?"

I listened and asked a handful of questions, jarred wide awake by the request from the voice on the other end. It wasn't bad news at all; in fact, it was an extraordinary opportunity with divine timing. The caller was one of the greatest leaders I have ever met in my life, my spiritual father, Bishop T. D. Jakes. Since moving back to Texas to pastor the north campus of The Potter's House (an extension of Bishop Jakes's church) in the Dallas area, I'd enjoyed frequent communication with him about the church and our shared ministry. He was calling to ask if I could take his place the following morning and deliver the closing keynote message for ManPower, his annual conference ministering to the needs of men. There was a death in the church and he felt it was very important that he be there for the family. The words were barely out of his mouth before I nearly dropped the phone. I sputtered, "Uhhh, of course, Bishop . . . if you need me to . . . I mean, are you sure you want *me* to do this?"

Yes, he was sure. He made it clear to me that this would be the first time a woman had ever spoken in the history of ManPower. This year's attendance was well over ten thousand—men of every race and economic bracket who had come from across the country and around the world to hear Bishop Jakes, along with a host of special guests, provide life-changing inspiration and practical wisdom.

My head was spinning, and my heart was racing. He said he had thought through his invitation and believed I was ready for such a new frontier. The reassurance in his voice was all I really needed, so I accepted his invitation, thanked him for such a great opportunity, and hung up the phone. Somehow I knew instantly that this was one of those sovereign shifting moments in my life. It was like a whirlwind, and it was all happening in the middle of the night. While I was fast asleep, God was making space for me in a new sphere of ministry! This would be a higher level than I had experienced before, but God knew it was in me. He was the One opening doors.

My fears pinballed inside my anxious mind, bouncing around the many potential negative consequences of my decision. Despite the frantic thoughts racing inside me, I felt stuck. I was willing, but I knew this opportunity was so much bigger than anything I'd ever done. The very idea was, well, crazy! The whole notion seemed surreal, as if I'd stepped into someone else's life. How did I, Sheryl Brady, a middle-aged woman with no formal training or seminary degree, a wife, mother, and grandmother, find herself about to address an international audience of thousands of Christian men?

This was either sovereign or suicidal. The spirit in me knew things would be okay; however, the human part of me was wrestling with my inadequacies. If I sound conflicted, I was! One thing I did know: the hand of God had steadily guided my life up until now. He had ordered my steps all of my life, and even those that he didn't order, he worked them all in together for my good!

As I pondered the possibilities before me, my mind shifted to the first time I ever encountered Bishop Jakes. Little had I known, almost twenty years earlier, where it would lead when I decided to attend a weekend worship service to hear a preacher whose message had already changed me forever.

It had to have been a record-breaking scorcher that summer day in Cleveland, Ohio. The temperature felt 100 degrees outside, and at least 150 degrees inside the church, where I sat fanning and frustrated. At the last minute, I had decided to drive into the city so I could hear the preacher who had recently ignited my faith with a combustible passion to know God unlike anything I'd ever experienced.

A pastor friend had given me a couple of tapes by Bishop T. D. Jakes, an up-and-coming preacher from West Virginia. My friend thought I would be blessed by the powerful messages, but he had failed to warn me that it would be hazardous to listen and drive simultaneously. Bishop Jakes's messages have a way of "wrecking" people, and they don't discriminate when or where they hit you. Whether you hear him in a beautiful church setting or while behind the wheel, you feel as though Bishop Jakes has been following you around the house all week long! He connects to the deepest parts of you, letting you know that God is real! (Some of you are smiling right now because you're just as guilty as I am of trying to drive and have church at the same time!) Bishop Jakes's preaching delivered the salt of the Gospel with so much flavor that I became thirsty—no, parched—for what he had in God. So when the opportunity presented itself for me to experience his ministry in person, I knew I had to be there.

Despite the unbearable heat, the building was full of saints who were intent on having church. And have it we did! We had church, more church, and nothing but church, so help me God! First, we offered praise and worship, and then we lifted up worship and praise. After praise and worship, and worship and praise, we were blessed by praise dancers. After praise and worship, and worship and praise, and praise dancers, we enjoyed a play by a visiting ministry.

Don't get me wrong, it was a wonderful experience, but after several hours of the unbearable heat, the hard wooden pews, the stuffy air in a crowded sanctuary, and the lateness of the hour—well, I was done! It was nearly 10 P.M., and Bishop Jakes had not even gotten started yet! As my patience shifted from thin to threadbare, I saw the man who had ushered me before the throne of God step to the pulpit.

Needless to say, the impact was life-changing. Bishop's message gave me hope during a season when I felt hopeless, helpless, and numb, wondering if God really had a plan for my life. My natural circumstances were no different after he had finished preaching, yet something in my spirit came alive. Something woke up in me. For the first time, I could see myself potentially surviving what I thought was a derailed destiny. His words pierced my heart and flooded my soul with

God's power and love in ways I'd never experienced. I was literally on the floor by the time the evening was over! Overwhelmed with feelings that God had invaded the room and was talking directly to me, I knelt down and prayed, experiencing a very private moment in a very public place. I actually got to meet Bishop Jakes that night after the service (more than making up for my heated impatience!), and it was the first of many times our paths crossed.

My husband and I continued down the road of full-time ministry that we had been on prior to my encountering Bishop Jakes. Thanks to divine appointments, we kept running into Bishop at conferences, revivals, and special worship services. I would often provide special music or lead the praise and worship portion of the services we shared together. Our families developed a friendship grounded in our desire to know and serve God. Throughout the many milestones of ministry (I'll share more about my journey in chapters to come), my husband and I always remained in contact with Bishop Jakes. One step led to another, and twenty years later, my family and I had moved our ministry, our kids, our grandkids, and all our earthly possessions back to Texas from Raleigh, North Carolina, to work alongside this man that I almost missed meeting all those years before.

Reflecting on how God had brought our paths together and set us on a course full of blessings, I marveled at how God had orchestrated what he knew all along. As surprised and disoriented as I felt at the prospect of closing ManPower in Bishop's absence, God wasn't the least bit surprised. Before the foundations of the world were established, God, in all of his wisdom, intertwined our lives and ministries in such a way to strengthen, encourage, and support one another. I had no idea, running into that little church on a steamy night in Cleveland all those years ago, that God would ultimately lead me onto a runway that would launch me into places, pulpits, and positions I would never have dreamed possible!

THE MEMORY MADE ME SMILE. YES, IF GOD WANTED ME to speak at ManPower and deliver his message to the hungry hearts of so many men, then he would have to supersize whatever I had to offer. I would need more than what I could provide alone. So I prayed and reminded God that he would have to provide me with whatever I lacked so he would be honored and the men in attendance would be blessed.

After several minutes pouring out my heart before God, I knew without a doubt that the invitation came from him and not just Bishop Jakes. I experienced a calm sense of God's presence and his blessing on me. I knew I might not have all I needed to do the job, but I also knew that the One, who continued to surprise me with his goodness, faithfulness, and presence, no matter where my life's adventure led, would never let me walk into something this big without holding my hand.

Returning my phone to its charger on my nightstand, I smiled to myself. No wonder it had seemed so far away, so out of reach when it began ringing—my world had shifted, and nothing would ever be the same again! Knowing that I needed more rest if I was to do my best the following day, I went back to bed and, much to my surprise, slept soundly the rest of the night. I've always believed that the greatest faith move is when you can rest in what God has promised you, and I was blessed to experience it that night. Sometimes you just have to tell the devil, "I'm going to bed!" because you have such peace with God. So that's exactly what I did!

The next day flashed by in swirls of fluid motion that reminded me of watching the changing patterns of a kaleidoscope. Bishop Jakes had decided not to announce the identity of his replacement, only promising a surprise guest. While some men would stay until the closing session, I feared that once they saw me up on the stage of the convention center, they would head for the exits.

In fact, my presence had just the opposite effect. When I was introduced, men who had been browsing through books in the lobby and taking a break began returning to their seats. If anyone left, it was hard to tell from where I was standing; the place appeared to be packed. Over ten thousand men, all expecting to hear Bishop T. D. Jakes rouse them with a soul-stirring conclusion, had decided to stay and hear the first woman ever to address a ManPower crowd.

The Lord's presence was abundantly evident.

As I took the podium and began to preach, I felt his power energize me and his Spirit lead me. Drawing on the life of Abraham, I explored the way God created a "trust fund" through the investment of faith capital—all the promises that God made to Abraham and kept. These miracles, gifts, and blessings became a sustaining source of hope for Abraham when all other resources dried up.

The same is true today, and available to all of us, I explained, and in our uncertain times of economic upheaval, career free fall, and fearful futures, it's imperative for us to remember the riches we have in the trust fund our Father has established for us. When we feel we are up against a wall, backed into a corner, and pushed over the edge, we can know that God will not only catch us but also cradle us in the palms of his hands. (And it was clear to me, if not to the men in attendance, that I was definitely relying that day on the resources of God's faithfulness from my own trust fund!)

As I concluded my message, I encouraged men to come to the altar and renew their faith, receive prayer from other men, and unburden their hearts. The response was overwhelming! Thousands of men crowded the area as tears flowed, secrets were shared, and needs were expressed. It had nothing to do with me other than my willingness to show up and be God's messenger. I didn't know I had it in me, but God knew and delighted in surprising me with another glimpse of who he made me to be.

As my memory of first meeting Bishop Jakes testifies, my pinnacle moment at ManPower did not happen overnight. In fact, it didn't happen in a matter of days, weeks, or months. It took *years* for God to prepare me for this opportunity. Most of the time, I wasn't able to see what he was up to or understand why certain events didn't unfold the way I wanted them to. But he knew where he was leading me. Each time we trust him with another layer of our lives, we discover more of the buried treasure of our true identities. God often allows us to surprise ourselves if we're willing to trust him one step at a time.

His Word promises we have everything we need to get through whatever comes our way. As Paul expressed so clearly, "I can do all things through Christ who strengthens me" (Phil. 4:13 NKJV). Often we don't even realize what we're capable of doing until a situation requires it of us.

Most of us never know the extent of our abilities until we're tested by adversity. You've probably heard about the way the human body can kick into overdrive during a crisis and perform incredible feats of strength, stamina, and resilience: the mother who is able to lift the car fender to free her trapped toddler; the firefighter who ignores the searing pain of his own injuries to rescue the unconscious resident of a blazing structure; the exhausted doctor who refuses to take a break, so she can try to save one more trauma patient. In each case, the individual had no idea what he or she was capable of doing until it was revealed by sheer necessity.

I'm convinced our spiritual lives operate in much the same way. Most of us have no idea what we are truly capable of accomplishing—or perhaps more accurately, what God has created us to achieve, with him as our power source. It usually takes a crisis situation or unexpected opportunity to crystallize the core substance of our true identity. We tend to avoid faith-testing trials and uncomfortable circumstances if given a choice—life's much easier without conflict and inconvenient surprises.

However, those mind-bending, heart-wrenching, faith-stretching moments often become the crucible in which our talents are forged into a tool that would never have existed otherwise. Once we realize our hidden strengths, then the tool joins others in our arsenal and becomes sharper and more resilient with each use. You never know when God will present you with an extraordinary invitation to discover more of the treasure buried inside you.

In this book, I want to explore the lives of the Bible's most talented, faithful, and amazing people and reveal that they

didn't know they had it in them either—not until God revealed the truth about their identities and abilities to them,
often in the midst of perilous trials and challenging situations.
How could Ruth have believed that she had the courage to
start over after losing everything? How could a humble shepherd boy understand that inside him was a slayer of giants?

Like these heroes of our faith, all of us have unclaimed
abilities waiting to be discovered. God wants to peel away the
layers that we often try to hide behind, dissolve the excuses
that we use as camouflage, and reveal the beauty of our true
selves. By sharing my own journey as well as examples from
history and current culture, I challenge you to reconsider the
way you see yourself and to reframe your understanding of
why you are here.

Do you know what you're made of? More important, do
you want to discover the many strengths dormant inside you
just waiting to be discovered? My hope is that you will be
inspired to reconsider your current challenges as opportunities for self-discovery and faith-enrichment. My prayer is
that you will finish this book and have a new perspective on
all God has brought you through, a greater awareness of all
you've accomplished and endured, and a revelation of confidence that comes from excavating the buried treasure within
your soul. May God illuminate your life through these pages
so that you can truly proclaim, "I didn't know I had it in me,
but now I do!"

CHAPTER ONE

THE GRACE TO START OVER

MY LIFE OFTEN SEEMS TO REVOLVE AROUND MOVING. Sometimes when I see the boxes in our garage, I can't remember if they are there for me to pack or unpack! And I know my experience has become the norm. As technology makes us more mobile, we're used to moving from state to state, country to country, to advance our careers, keep our jobs, or be closer to the people we love. Perhaps it's not the physical act of moving that's unsettling so much as the context of why we're moving.

Most of my moves have centered around my relationship with God and commitment to serve his church. In the introduction, I shared how I first met Bishop T. D. Jakes and indicated what an immediate, powerful impact he had on my spiritual journey. In fact, the outcome of that meeting in Cleveland on that hot summer night was the move my family made a few years later to Charleston, West Virginia, to serve with his ministry.

We were elders and elated to be a part of the church, but I must confess, I think we *took* much more than we *gave*. Not that we weren't givers, because we were, are, and always will be givers, but what we gave in terms of our time, talent, and treasure could in no way compare to that which we received in our spirits. I was hungry and thirsty for God, and week after week I would pull my chair up to the table that Bishop had spread and eat until I couldn't hold any more. God called us there, and for that I will eternally be grateful.

This move began a wonderful season for me and my family. The people were kind and welcoming. Our home in Charleston was very comfortable. Being born and raised in Detroit, I never would have thought I'd be so happy living in the hills of West Virginia, but I was! Due to our schedule of constant traveling to preach and sing, we hadn't had a home in a while, so just having our own place was refreshing. We had been in full-time ministry at this point for almost thirteen years, most of which was spent traveling. On top of it all, I got to sit under the teaching of the man who woke up things in me that I didn't even know were there!

A few years later, Bishop Jakes shared the calling God had placed on him to move his ministry to Texas, in the Dallas–Fort Worth area. Along with several other families, we pulled out boxes, packed, and made the trek west, becoming a part of The Potter's House.

Exactly one week later, with pieces of my life divided up into a gazillion boxes, I stood at the podium and opened the first service of a record-breaking, history-making ministry in a word of prayer. I still do not recall how I ended up being the one asked to do such an important task. And I will never forget how honored I was to be there and experience the awesomeness of that moment! Could it get any better than that? I was in a great church, serving with a great leader who was carrying a great Word, living in a great city—life was just, well, great!

After a few years, my husband, with whom I've worked hand in hand in ministry for the last thirty-four years, started getting that "I'm hearing from God look" in his eyes. Surely not! Why? Where? What for? Not that I was rebellious, but I just wanted to understand. Just a little bit of *explanation* would make *cooperation* a whole lot easier! As he talked and I cried, he said God had put it in his heart to go back east.

He made a statement to me I couldn't understand at the

time, but I've never forgotten it: "Baby, I need to get you out of here, because if I don't, you'll never become who God has called you to be." Looking back, I see that it was time for me to put all I had learned to work. As long as I just stayed there, eating from his table, I would never have gotten the hands-on experience I needed. It was as if I'd been in a twelve-year internship, and it was finally time for me to live out all that had been poured into me over the many years that I learned from this great ministry. With Bishop's blessing, we pulled out of the great state of Texas with our children, our dogs, our boxes, and a sense of purpose we couldn't even describe.

I felt a little like Abram when God spoke to him to leave his country and his kin, and then journey "to a place I will show thee" (Gen. 12:1). We were taking every step by faith and ultimately our *faithwalk* led us straight into Faith World Church in beautiful Orlando, Florida, under the leadership of Pastor Clint Brown. We knew this would be a temporary landing spot for us, where we would continue to wait upon the Lord for his direction. We knew he had planted a desire in us to build a church of our own; however, we were not exactly sure at the time where it would be.

Pastor Clint and the entire Faith World family were a great blessing to us. They welcomed us with open arms. They loved us, made space for us, encouraged and laughed with us, and helped us believe in "us." Pastor Clint has reckless faith. He built such faith in us regarding the gifting of

God in our lives that it wasn't long before we felt as if we were "well able to take the land" (Num. 13:30). The Lord began to put the city of Raleigh, North Carolina, on my husband's heart.

With all of the Word Bishop Jakes had planted in us, the faith Pastor Brown poured into us, and the prayers our family had prayed over us, we gathered up our kids, our dogs, and our boxes, and set out once again with an inexplicable grace to start over! Every step of the way we saw the provision and the protection of the Lord. Once we made it to Raleigh, we settled in for ten wonderful years, during which we founded The River Church. I was honored to co-lead and guide this baby through its infancy into a beautiful, mature community of believers. We'd never had to use as much faith as we had to use there, yet we'd never seen as much favor as we were shown there either.

On the very day of our tenth anniversary at The River, my husband and I were sitting at the dinner table with Bishop Jakes, and he began talking about vision. He shared with us how God speaks and brings a shift to his life, seemingly every ten years. Needless to say, he had my attention simply because this was exactly where I found myself, at a major milestone on my journey. I didn't say anything about it at the time, but somehow I knew this conversation was not one that we haphazardly stumbled into. Somehow I knew there was something seriously sovereign about the moment I had found myself in. Somehow I knew a significant shift was about to take place in our lives.

After dinner I thanked Bishop and his wife for their beautiful spirit of hospitality and we left Dallas, returning to North Carolina with an unexplainable excitement. What was God up to?

My eyes hadn't seen it, my ears hadn't heard it, but my Spirit knew that God was about to jet-propel us once again into his divine purpose for our lives. Sure enough, less than three weeks later my phone rang, and Bishop Jakes was on the line. "Sheryl, I'd like to ask you and Joby [my husband] to pray about coming home to Texas." He shared with us his vision to establish a campus extension in North Dallas that would be part of The Potter's House. At the end of our conversation, Joby and I thanked him for offering us such an awesome opportunity, assuring him we would pray for the perfect will of God to be made manifest. Hanging up the phone, I couldn't help but wonder if what I heard was actually what he said.

Could this really be God's plan for our lives? Could God really be asking us to return to Dallas? Was it his will for us to leave North Carolina? Out of everyone in the world Bishop Jakes could've called, he called us? It was one of those rare times I felt speechless and knew that I had to spend some major time alone with God in order to sort through the swirling emotions inside. We needed to hear his voice.

We needed to know that, once again, he would give us the grace to start over.

Her feet were so tired, and yet she knew there were many miles to go before they would reach the border. Dust hovered above the road and choked her, making her more aware of her thirst. How could her life have changed so quickly?

For a while they had all been so happy together, so grateful to have formed a new family. It seemed like just days ago Ruth had been sitting with her husband, his brother and wife, and her mother-in-law and enjoying a meal of bread and fish. Her husband's father had died many years before, but they had endured their grief, grateful that he had saved their lives from the terrible famine in their homeland. Even though she hadn't conceived a child yet, there was still much joy and hope for the future. Ruth and her husband looked ahead with anticipation.

And then the worst happened. He didn't come home from the sea one afternoon, and then an old man came and brought them the terrible news. Her husband was dead. Before the shock of his passing could fade, the unimaginable struck again, and her brother-in-law drew his last breath as well. She and her sister-in-law, Orpah, and mother-in-law, Naomi, consoled each other as best they could, but the double blow felt unbearable. Naomi wailed and sobbed with such anguish.

Now they walked in silence, the three of them. Naomi had decided that she would return to her home in Bethlehem, where the Lord was providing food for the Israelites. The woman who had become like a second mother to Ruth worked hard each day to contain the wells of gut-wrenching grief, anger, and bitterness that ran so deep. Ruth herself continued to grieve, but what choice did she have but to go forward? Everyone told her that she was young and would marry again and bear children, but she wasn't sure. After what had happened to them, nothing was certain anymore. (Ruth 1)

Perhaps of all my moves, returning to Dallas from North Carolina was the hardest. I can't even begin to articulate all of the thoughts that raced through my mind over the next months after Bishop Jakes's phone call. Going to The Potter's House would be wonderful, but leaving The River and the beautiful people who taught me how to pastor in the first place would be, needless to say, extremely painful.

I'm guessing you've been there, too. When you are faced with a decision, an opportunity, a choice about your life's direction, it's so tempting to stay put and maintain a comfortable pace on level ground. As we get older (certainly as I get older!), it seems harder to pack up and start over, more challenging to transplant the tender roots so newly established and reimmerse them in distant soil. While the grassy ground often looks greener on the other side, by middle age most of us have learned that beneath the beautiful emerald turf we sometimes find the soil rocky and barren, inhospitable to our attempts at going deep.

From my experience, and I'm guessing yours, moving always poses innumerable risks and countless questions: *Will it be worth leaving what I know I have here, for the possibility of what I might have there? Will my new home be as comfortable and enjoyable as my present one? Will the people there accept me and my family, welcoming us as part of their community and fellowship? Or will we find ourselves locked into the role of outsiders, always kept at arm's length from the locals, the natives, the long-term community members who know they belong and want to keep their circle closed?*

What will the future hold for us in this new land? Will the blessing that's so obviously on our lives go with us? Will the goodness of the Lord taste as good to us in Texas as it does in North Carolina? Am I even capable of doing this? These were the questions I asked myself. These were the questions that I honestly needed answers to.

Knowing that answers emerge from experience, I went to my Bible, the greatest book ever written. I was immediately reminded of a couple of dear friends of mine. I've never met them in person, but through the power of their story re-corded in God's Word, I've learned so much about what it means to love well, to commit, to obey, and to be faithful. Ruth and Naomi remind me that any move begins with our hearts and not our feet. Their story is one of having more courage than common sense, more love than logic, and more faith than fear.

THE SCENE WOULD ALWAYS HAUNT HER. STANDING IN the middle of the road with Orpah and Naomi, Ruth watched as her dear sister-in-law returned to Moab, back to her family there. Naomi had insisted. They had stopped beside a well to drink and refresh themselves, the water so cold on their parched throats.

And then suddenly, her second mother began speaking softly to them. As tears crawled down the older woman's withered cheeks, Naomi told her sons' wives that they must continue with her no farther. Orpah was torn, clearly, but she finally relented and walked back the way they had come.

Change did not come easily for Orpah. She was definitely the fruit of her homeland, Moab, a name that meant "the place that doesn't require change" (see Jer. 48:11). And while she loved Naomi and had been greatly influenced by her God, when the moment of truth came, Orpah couldn't make a clean break from her past because she found change to be too challenging. Severing old ties and launching into unknown territories was a price she was for me, because I'm usually the stabilizer,

everyone is doing well. My grandson Jade

reinforced his sweet but weary voice whe

GeGe. I didn't take my nap." As with all

tine had been shattered.

Finally it was time to turn off the l

place that we had known as home for so

daughter Lana and I flipped the basemen

ticed in the corner her beautiful little da

had found a crib mattress that somehow

the moving truck. She sat there with her

ing against the wall.

I said, "Kenzie, what's wrong, baby?"

She mumbled, "I don't want to leave.

Lana fell on the crib mattress next to

gallon of long overdue, locked-up tears. S

tiful girls sitting there crying made me

three generations of crybabies, huddle

boxed-up basement. So we just let oursel

Finally, we headed upstairs and made a

in the midst of an unbelievable, torrent

the sky was crying that night.

As I was trying to get the car turned

headlights shining on the dumpster we

carding trash and debris. We had sent an

ing to Goodwill, so everything in the

unprepared to pay. And while standing at the border of a break-through, she kissed them good-bye, forever turning her back on Ruth, Naomi, and Naomi's God.

As Ruth stood watching Orpah, for just a moment, questions flooded her mind: Could she really start over in a strange land where she would know no one except Naomi? Should she go back with Orpah and return to what was familiar, the people and place she knew so well? And what about this God of her husband and his family? Was he in the midst of her journey, or was he abandoning her to find her own way?

One glance at Naomi's face, the wrinkles of worry and the eyes of emptiness, and Ruth knew that returning to Moab was not an option. Her questions did not matter. There was nothing Naomi could say that could compel Ruth to abandon her. She had told Naomi that she loved her and that she had even discovered a love for this strange Hebrew God, the one Naomi herself struggled to trust, now that her husband and sons had been taken. Naomi tried to insist, tried to gently push Ruth away, but she would have none of it.

"Ms. Naomi, I can't go back. I have nothing to go back for. Things are different now. Knowing you has changed my life. I was incomplete without you. I found God in you and from there I found purpose. Yes, Ms. Naomi, you were the one who connected me to my destiny! You told me who I was. You told me what I could become. You woke up the sleeping things that were inside of me. I'm awake now and it's all because of you! How in the world do you think I

could go back to sleep now? Whatever I'v...
Whatever I've got to change, I'll change it,...
where I am! My heart is fixed.

"*Wherever you go, I'm going. Whereve...*
living. And whenever we've walked togethe...
wherever you die is where I want to die. An...
down, I want them to leave a spot for me ri...

"*Ms. Naomi, I don't know where we ar...*
est, it really doesn't matter. If we are sta...
what? We are doing it together!"

HAVE YOU EVER HAD TO TAKE A ...
someone you loved? If not a physical r...
the heart? Have you ever had to choo...
safe and walking in uncharted territory...
even though I had moved many times...
stood out.

Moving day was finally here—time...
Carolina and head back home to Texa...
and their spouses and kids were movi...
and me. Together, we had spent the last...
hurricane of movers, boxes, tape, and...
Each of us, in our own way, showed th...
the-world-is-going-on syndrome. This...

broken or beyond repair. It was now overflowing, and there on top was Jaden's first set of drums. A born drummer, my grandson had progressed from toy drums and was now on his second set of real drums—but who's counting!

In the blink of an eye, the dumpster became a stage and my headlights became spotlights focused right on Jaden's drums. And then it hit me like a ton of bricks: we were leaving them behind! In fact, I was leaving a whole era of my life behind. Between the tears and the ridiculous rain, I don't know how we made it out of there in one piece. I felt as if I was driving away from the best ten years of my life—not to mention my eighty-two-year-old mother, who I was leaving wrapped up warm in the arms of my sweet sister, just a few miles down the road. Zipping in and out for those "I need my mommy" moments would not be so easy from Dallas.

Tears of pain and pleasure streamed down my face. As the joy and sorrow poured out of me, I couldn't tell which tear was which. I could only say, "Lord, my heart is full of gratitude!" I was grateful for faithfulness, family, and future, resting in the knowledge that at that moment God had plans for us under the lock and key of his sovereignty.

Whether you're familiar with Ruth's story or not, I believe we all know how scary it can be to move from one place to another. It's not just exchanging the familiar for the unknown; moving forces us to look within ourselves and find more strength than we knew we had, more courage than we've ever displayed before, and more faith in the goodness of our loving Father than we've ever had to show.

Sometimes we have to move in order to survive. Even when it's too risky, it's still tempting to stay where we are. You don't have to take the promotion; you can just stay with the position you have and the job security that it provides. If you go up the ladder at work, there's always a chance you could fall even further if you fail. But can you live with the questions that will forever gnaw at your peace? The questions that will creep into your mind at the end of the day as you're attempting to sleep: *I wonder if I would have been even more successful if I'd taken that job? I wonder if our family would've been happier if we'd moved? What if God had something special for me in that new place that I was too afraid to take hold of? What if I've missed a blessing by being blinded by my fears?*

Each of us has a choice every day either to remain in the Moab of our lives, the place with people just like us, the place where we've always belonged, the place that makes no real demands on us, or to embark on a journey of faith into a new country. Naomi was compelled to return to her homeland because of the dire circumstances she experienced in Moab, but her daughter-in-law Ruth clearly had a choice.

Or did she? Reading between the lines, I think something in her said, *Why should I sit here and die when I can leave here and live?* What did Orpah miss by not trekking to Bethlehem with her sister- and mother-in-law? What—or whom—would she have discovered in the grain fields of the future?

THE AFTERNOON SUN BEAT DOWN ON HER BACK AS SHE stooped to gather the grain that had been spilled in the fields of Naomi's kinsman, Boaz. He had been so kind to her, so gentle, so different from what she expected. She had bowed her head in respect and kept her eyes lowered, but he had spoken to her directly, treating her not like a foreigner, a Moabite, but like a real person, like a woman. His workers also treated her with the same kindness and respect, offering her water to drink. She suspected they even were spilling more grain than usual just so she would be able to gather plenty.

She dared not say it out loud to Naomi, but Ruth felt a new hope in her heart, a new dream taking shape. Could it be that in this foreign land with the Hebrews her heart could find a home? In the quiet of the evening, or sometimes when she was alone in the fields, she would hear the Lord speak to her. He was unlike any god she had ever encountered back in Moab, but she was glad. This God was real. And he cared about her and Naomi. Ruth knew that he was the reason they had a place to live and food to eat. She gave thanks in her heart. (Ruth 2)

* * *

HAVE YOU EVER NOTICED THE WAY GOD PROVIDES FOR us when he challenges us to make moves in life? It may not be easy and we may get weary, and even exhausted, from the journey, but when we follow him, our Father will always sustain us. Just as God promises to remain with us, he also promises to take care of our needs.

Whether it's manna for our daily bread or crumbs for the sparrows, our Father loves to provide life-giving gifts for his children. Ruth's story reveals even more of God's provision as the two women settled into the community and discovered that one of Naomi's relatives by marriage, Boaz, was a wealthy landowner with many fields of grain. Can you look back on your life and remember the times God has provided for you and your family? Ways he has surprised you with unexpected blessings at times of extraordinary need?

When we stay in familiar places, it's so tempting to get in a rut and overlook all that God gives us. We start taking things for granted—our homes, our jobs, our families, our health. But when we're following God's call on our lives, we're forced to rely on Him for everything. We're forced to recognize the many ways he provides even the smallest things for us.

Having moved several times in my life, I've come to appreciate what it means to discover things that I can so easily take for granted—a grocery store close to my house, a good dentist, a good school nearby when my children were young, natural beauty unique to each particular setting. What have you been taking for granted in your life? If you were to pause and make a list of a dozen things that you're especially grateful for today, what would you put on it? Fresh strawberries? A car that runs? The ability to walk around the block with your child? A job you enjoy? A family who loves you? I challenge you to make such a list and consider the "spilled grain" that God is currently scattering into your life!

Ruth crouched in the shadows near the rear corner of the threshing room. The place smelled of wheat and barley, a rich, earthy scent that held the promise of nourishment and life. She couldn't believe she was actually acting so boldly—surely she would never have been so bold back in Moab. When she had met Naomi's son back home, it had been so easy, so natural. Yes, he was a foreigner, but he seemed to know her so well.

Now, she was doing something she had never done before. She was taking such a huge risk, going against what others (even those back home) would consider proper. But somehow this entire move had been about taking risks, about following the voice of her new God, the one who continued to provide for her and talk her through the risky places in life. Was it really possible that he might give her this handsome, kind man as her second husband? Could she really be so blessed to have two men in her life love her with such care and tenderness?

She remained quiet, hidden in the darkness, as Boaz finished eating and drinking and reclined on a pallet on the floor only a few feet away from her. Soon his even breathing and tiny snores were the only sounds in the room. Only the moonlight streaming in a high window allowed her to see him sleeping so peacefully. Silently, she tiptoed to the end of his pallet and knelt down. Lifting the light wool blanket, she uncovered his feet and then reclined on the floor beside them. Was it possible to love someone she had only just met?

She must have drifted off. Now she had heard something, a sound like a man's voice. Where was she? Oh, no! Ruth remembered as she looked up at Boaz only to find him wide awake, staring at her.

"Who are you, woman? And what are you doing here?" he asked her in his deep, soft voice.

"I am your servant, Ruth," she whispered and removed the veil covering most of her face. "As the kinsman-redeemer of Naomi's family, please cover me with your garment."

He hesitated and Ruth thought she heard him making a sound like laughter. Finally, Boaz said, "You have blessed me and must be a gift from the Lord. You may stay here until morning and then we will sort things out."

Ruth breathed a sigh of relief and felt tears well up in her eyes. The presence of the Lord was there in the room with the two of them. She was exactly where she was supposed to be. (Ruth 3)

* * *

WHAT RISK DO YOU NEED TO TAKE TODAY IN ORDER TO experience the blessing God has for you next? What opportunity is calling you to take bold steps in its direction? What's the next step on the journey toward the abundant life for which you were created? As Naomi discovered, it's never too late to allow God to redeem our losses and surprise us with blessings beyond our imagination. Upon returning home, she had told her old friends to call her Mara, a name that means "bitter" (Ruth 1:20). She wanted everyone to know she had suffered unbearable losses and that she wasn't going to dare hope for anything from anyone.

But through the loyalty and the risk-taking of her devoted daughter-in-law Ruth, Naomi discovered that her story was not finished. God could and did provide for her more than she herself could've dreamed. It wasn't too late for her, and it's not too late for you. No matter what you've lost, no matter who's left you, no matter where you find yourself, God can and will surprise you with his grace if you'll only let him.

THE BABY AT HER BREAST SMILED AND COOED EVEN WHEN she handed him off to his grandmother. Ruth had never seen Naomi radiating such joy and delight—not even when her sons had been alive. The Lord had shown them so much favor. And so much of his lovingkindness came through her husband, Boaz.

The days when Ruth had felt weary with grief melted into the past. She had stepped into her future, and all she could do was give thanks and praise. If not for remaining with Naomi, she would've missed the greatest blessings of her life. One cheek-to-cheek brush with her new baby boy, and she knew every risk she had ever taken was well worth it.

IT'S NOT JUST A HAPPY ENDING FOR NAOMI AND RUTH, although it's wonderfully inspiring to see all they went through and how God provided for them. It's good news for us as well. Because the last thing we're told in the book of Ruth, slipped in very matter-of-factly as just another detail, packs a real punch.

We're told Boaz and Ruth's son is named Obed (Ruth 4:17), who became the father of Jesse, who was the father of David. In case we miss it, the book spells out the genealogy, clearly emphasizing that this is the line of David, the shepherd boy chosen by God himself and anointed as Israel's king.

And it's not only that Ruth was kicking off the royal lineage for future kings, because, as you may recall, the family tree of David bore the fruit of a baby in a manger named Jesus, the Messiah and God's own Son, who came to be the ultimate kinsman-redeemer of us all. We see Ruth's name mentioned again in the genealogy of Christ in the New Testament (Matt. 1:5), a feat in itself, since women's names were rarely, if ever, listed in this patriarchal culture, which relied on the father line.

The message then is extraordinary for us today, not only because of all that Ruth endured and then had redeemed by the Lord's lovingkindness, but also because she was an outsider. The last person an Israelite would have picked to be the great-great-grandmother of the Messiah was a Moabite. Through her kindness, tenacity, obedience, and, above all, her willingness to risk time and again, Ruth provided a model for all of us who are required to move.

And the reality, my friend, is that all of us are called to move in life—if not literally, then metaphorically as part of our journey of transformation. We cannot remain where we are, "the place that never changes," if we seek to follow God's will for our lives and experience the fullness of his many blessings.

Ruth was willing to meet life as it came to her. She risked by marrying a foreigner, by committing to leave her homeland, by committing to her mother-in-law when there was no longer a husband/son to bind them, by not knowing what she would find in Bethlehem, by picking up grain in the fields, by sleeping at Boaz's feet. My hope for you is to experience God's presence no matter what you may be going through or where he calls you to move.

You may not know it, but you have everything you need to take the next step. You may not know you have it in you, but, like Ruth, others whom God has placed in your life do know it. Accept their love and support and allow God to reveal to you what they already see.

Maybe you need to let go of old hurts or grieve past losses in order to move forward. Maybe you need to be patient and obedient and keep doing what God asks of you. I don't know what your issue might be, the thing that might have tears running down your face, have you pacing the floors in the midnight hour, wondering what is next. But I do know that God knows and has equipped you with everything you need to move through it and begin again.

If you aren't sure about your next move or which direction to go in, ask him. He is your father, and he will always have your best interest at heart. He will never abandon you, and he is with you right now, even as your eyes scan the words on this page. No matter what you are going through, he knows what you need.

As we prepare to move on to the next chapter, let me leave you with this: destiny doesn't happen *in spite of us*, destiny happens *because of us*. There are things that you and I must do to provoke the release of God's purpose in our lives. We may not know all of what God has placed within us, but we must be open to find it and, against all odds, continue to move forward.

I can't wait to meet this gutsy girl one day and thank her for making a decision that has affected all of us. You see, Ruth had to leave Moab not only for *herself,* she had to leave because of what was *in her.* Locked inside of a woman, who was locked up inside of Moab, was Jesus, the one who has given all of us the grace to start over.

CHAPTER TWO

TREASURE IN A TRAMP'S HOUSE

THUD. THUD. THUD. SUCH FRANTIC POUNDING AT HER door. What time was it, anyway?

She was used to strangers knocking at all hours of the night. Most were men who had heard about her from gossip in the neighborhood or repeat customers who liked what she offered. Everyone knew her. She was well known for trading her body for money, food, and fine clothes. She wasn't just Rahab; she was Rahab the Harlot. A woman of the night. A woman whose name was always followed by her reputation.

It wasn't easy, but then, what job was? She knew that in order to practice her profession, she would have to learn the art of engaging without really being engaged, and that she did! She made a decision early in the game to be good at giving them her body without ever giving them her heart. She had locked down that part of her, promising herself never to give it to anyone. Just as she controlled who came in and went out of her front door, she would also control who came in and went out of her heart. It made her job easier. No emotions. No feelings and certainly no love. Just a business transaction. Just another day's journey.

A knock at her door in the midnight hour often awakened her but never alarmed her. This was nothing new to Rahab. Same song, second verse. At least that's what she thought. But one glance through the peephole of her front door and she knew something was different. These were foreigners, outsiders, Jews—and that could only mean trouble. She took a deep breath and wondered what she should do.

Word on the street had it that the Israelites had escaped Pharaoh's army. The whole town was talking about what had happened in Egypt when, out of nowhere, the Red Sea rolled back against its shores, opening a road for the Israelites to pass through on dry ground. When the very last one of them had crossed safely to the other side, the water returned, drowning the enemies that were chasing them.

And all of Jericho had heard about the plagues and the miracles. One thing was very clear: the Israelites were definitely being protected by someone bigger than themselves. Rahab had even heard rumors that their God had promised them Jericho—her homeland—and now they were standing at her front door! (Joshua 2)

HAVE YOU EVER BEEN GOING THROUGH A TYPICAL DAY when everything suddenly seemed to change in a matter of moments? Maybe it was a new customer coming through your office door. Maybe it was a casual conversation while waiting in line at the bank. It might have been someone unexpected knocking at your door! We tend to view these kinds of encounters as interruptions at best, or threats to our security at worst. In actuality, though, these are often opportunities to answer the call of God on our lives.

We may not know we have it in us, and God often has to surprise us into using what he's placed there. We may think it's too late for us or that we're not good enough, but the story of Rahab reminds us that there's always treasure inside us, no matter how tarnished we may feel on the outside.

I love Rahab's story because she presents us with all kinds of questions, all kinds of surprises, and all kinds of hope for anyone who's ever felt as if he or she was too dirty for God to love. Much more than just a prostitute with a heart of gold (you know, the kind in movies like *Pretty Woman*), Rahab was someone who definitely wasn't aware of her potential. She was strong and independent, a businesswoman who knew how to deal with tough customers. But she also longed for more—a life full of meaning and purpose, a life based on love and not on lust, on kindness and not currency.

Under the harshest of circumstances—war and the destruction of her hometown—she was quick on her feet, went with her gut, took a risk, saved the lives of her family as well as her own, and made history in the process. All because she trusted the Lord—this strange God whom the Jews brought with them.

Can you imagine what she must have felt standing at her door and seeing those dangerous spies asking to come in? I believe that despite all she'd heard, everything in her wanted to let them in immediately! Maybe what she'd heard wasn't true . . . maybe they weren't as bad as she'd been told. Perhaps Jehovah himself had led them, step by step, into the house of Rahab.

I'm not trying to be judgmental, but you can't help but wonder why, if God needed to use somebody, he didn't choose a nobler person than Rahab. Why did he pick her, of all people? Why her house? Was there not a more honorable house? Why not the governor's house? Why not the king's house? What would make a good God send his good men to a house like hers?

I'm convinced it was because he had already begun softening her heart. Did he know that if anyone in Jericho was ready for change, she was the one? One thing we know for sure is that when she looked out and saw the spies, she knew, beyond the shadow of a doubt, that these men did not come to her for the same reasons all the other men came!

Something leapt inside of her. This was definitely different. The knock she heard at the door was resounding in her spirit! Rahab the Harlot had an explosion of hope! Maybe those whispered conversations she had with the one man she couldn't see or touch were about to pay off. Maybe the one she had been crying out to secretly somehow understood the things she couldn't even say. Did he see that written between the lines of her life were the words *Help me, I'm trapped*?

I can just imagine what Rahab must have been feeling: *I don't know what life is like outside of this walled-up city called Jericho, but I am desperately ready to find out! There's got to be more for me! If not, then why am I living with this nagging feeling of discontentment? Why can't I just be happy? Why can't I just accept where I am? So, I have made some mistakes! Is it not possible to make a mistake and not be a mistake? I have failed, but does that make me a failure forever? And yes, I am a prostitute, but something inside of me knows that I still have purpose and potential, and, given a chance, I would show that there's so much more to me than meets the eye!*

Oh, this was one knock she *had* to answer! Deliverance

was at her door! Allowing these two men in meant she would finally find her way out! And without another moment's hesitation she welcomed those who had all of Jericho on high alert. Where the rest of the city saw impending judgment, Rahab saw a divine exit strategy!

Who is knocking at your door with an opportunity that you might initially view as a problem? Prayer often helps us discern. Could it be that what appears to be a dangerous conflict could really be a message of mercy from on high? Rahab certainly reminds us that no matter how many times or different ways we may have failed, God still hears our cries. He still pursues us and longs to use us. He still knocks at our door and wants to enter into our lives. We have to do our part and follow his instructions. We have to show good faith in trusting him. But he's there for us and wants to set us free even when everything around us is falling apart.

SHE HAD BARELY FINISHED LISTENING TO WHAT THE TWO *strangers had to say when she heard another sharp knock. "That's the king's messengers. They must know you are here. Quickly, run and hide yourselves up on the roof while I find a way to distract them." Very carefully she slid back the bolt on the door, anxious about what the men on the other side had to say.*

"Rahab, I have a message for you from the king."

She opened the door wider and nodded, indicating she was listening.

"The king is demanding that you turn over the two foreigners right now! They are spies! They have been sent to scout our defenses before they destroy us." The messenger paused to let his words sink in. "So hand them over—now!"

"Are you kidding me? Do you actually think I would be hiding spies? I don't have the slightest clue as to what you are talking about!" She swallowed hard, trying not to let her panic show. She could handle this; she had no choice. She was used to talking to men, making deals, and striking bargains. She knew she was playing with fire, but she was compelled to protect them.

The king's messenger glared at her as he sized up her story. "Rahab, listen to me. These men are dangerous. If they come back, or if you see them along the city walls, send someone to the palace right away."

"Yes, of course." She nodded like a good patriot and carefully shut the door, bolting it quickly behind her.

That had been too close for comfort! What was she thinking? Was she crazy for risking so much on a belief in the God of her country's enemy?

WHY WOULD A WOMAN IN RAHAB'S POSITION TAKE SUCH a risk? She was harboring her nation's enemy! How could she, of all people, do this to the only homeland she had ever known? Had it been anybody else, at any other time, she would surely have thrown them under the bus, right? But this time . . . well, something was different now.

God must surely have been working in her heart before their arrival. He had sent his own scouting party ahead by lighting a spark of hope in Rahab's heart. He had prepared her for these men. The look in their eyes and the sound of their voices had stirred something in her. They had awakened her to the truth that their God was the true and living God, and as long as he was for them, nothing would be able to withstand them. He was the Almighty! He was all-powerful! And he watched over his people with the eye of an eagle.

Hiding the spies was frightening and risky, but destiny was pulling Rahab like gravity! She was a gambler, and this time she was going for broke!

You see, I suspect that Rahab and the leaders in Jericho were allies. It seems reasonable to believe that she took care of them, and they took care of her. The king himself knew her by name. It's even possible the city did everything it could to make and keep her happy. She was likely an asset that brought great revenue into the city of Jericho. So they watched out for her, even gave her special housing arrangements, high upon the wall.

Despite all the money and favor she had with dignitaries

and clients that kept her living large in her house with a view, Rahab was still one very miserable woman. A woman who desperately longed for fulfillment, she had learned the hard way that it was something money could not buy!

I'm not sure what all she had withstood in life, but whatever it was, it likely left her cold and calloused. She may have been accommodating, warm, and gracious to her clients, but should you look a little deeper into her life, I suspect you would discover that in order to do this line of work consistently, one has to disconnect her emotions and cultivate a measure of callousness. Maybe you can identify. Perhaps, like her, you have had people assume that with a smile as contagious as yours, surely you've never had to cry. Or they glance your way and think that because you're attractive, you've never had to be alone. They may assume that someone with as many lovers as you've had probably doesn't know what it is like to need a human touch.

Yet only you know how many relationships you've lost. Only you know the abuse you've suffered at the hands of those who were supposed to love you and never harm you. Only you know the things that were said *to* you and *about* you that have haunted you every day of your life.

So many things that others say about us create false limitations. Often the things that were said in the past carry so much power that they shape our future. What we were told about ourselves then begins to control and limit us now.

Words that wounded you so severely in your past are now threatening to deny you your future.

Only you know the times you were overlooked, overshadowed, and overthrown by those you trusted. Only you know how you've poured your heart out over and over again while those to whom you were vulnerable shattered it into a million pieces, leaving you alone with the task of picking them up and finding the courage to start all over again.

Whatever Rahab had been through, it was really not that different from what many of us have been through. At the risk of offending you, I'm serious when I say that you and I are no better than this prostitute. Maybe we've chosen to take different roads and make different decisions, but at the end of the day, we've all made choices that have left us disappointed in others as well as in ourselves. The good news is Rahab's story allows us to see that for every *disappointment*, God has a *divine appointment*!

SHE HAD LOWERED THE RED CORD FROM THE WINDOW ON the top floor of her house just as the foreign spies had instructed her. It would be the sign of her deliverance, a signal to the advancing Hebrew army to spare her house. What if they had tricked her? What if the scarlet cord made no difference? No, it was their God who had told them to tell her about the scarlet cord. And he would honor his word.

When the foreign army descended and she heard the screams of neighbors, friends, men and women, children, braying donkeys, and bleating goats, it was more than she could bear. Her sadness was great. But her gratitude was greater. Because the more the noise and terrifying sobs and bloodshed rose from the streets, the more her confidence in the Lord grew. Her house was safe! No one came near it or even seemed to acknowledge its existence. She felt as if it must be invisible in the eyes of the Israelites.

Finally someone—one of the spies who had hidden earlier on her roof—came for her and her family. As the dust settled and the cries subsided and the blood dried on the streets of Jericho, Rahab and her mother and father, her brothers and sisters, were led outside by this man who had kept his promise to her, just as she had kept hers to him. They were treated kindly, respectfully, and kept clear of danger. They were led outside the shambles of the city walls and given a little camp of their own.

No matter what she had done with her life, Rahab the Harlot showed undeniably that she had been chosen by God! Now, you or I might not have chosen her, but he did! He knew all about her, yet he chose her. He knew every mistake she would ever make, yet he chose her. There was nothing anyone could tell him that would disqualify her, because he chose her.

All of her life's experiences were preparing her to be used by God. Every now and then, God chooses somebody unworthy, cleans her up, and sets her in a place of honor. Despite all the men who knew Rahab, and all the women who did not like her, God looked beyond her faults, saw her need, and still chose her!

In many ways, God did a total renovation on Rahab's life. He removed the thin layers of others' perceptions that had been pasted on her, took the foundation, which was stronger than she ever realized, and created something new. In fact, there are many amazing similarities between the city of Jericho and Rahab. First of all, though Jericho was inhabited by many evil people, it was property that had been earmarked as an inheritance for God's children. Those outside Israel who chose to make this city their home were trespassers. This was not their land. Rahab was not her own either. God had a plan for her from the very beginning.

Second, just as Jericho was "straightly shut up" (Josh. 6:1), so was Rahab. She also was protected by walls she erected, built from the incidents and accidents and trauma she'd endured. Walls are what you build when your heart has been broken and you are determined never to allow it to be in such a vulnerable place again. A wall is a defense mechanism you use to protect a home, a city, or a person from future pain.

Third, just as Jericho was full of treasure, so was Rahab! The problem is that for years the walls had hidden the treasure from everyone, including Rahab herself. However, one decision to open her home to the spies and her heart to their God started a revolution in her life. She couldn't explain it, and she didn't quite understand it, but something in her knew that she was born for more than to live and die as a prostitute in Jericho!

Somehow she had gotten a glimpse of God's bigger picture. Somehow she began to understand that this was not just about her, this was about what was *in* her! This was about generations to come! This was about her legacy!

For inside of Rahab was Boaz, and in Boaz was Obed, and in Obed was Jesse, who was the father of David, and in David there was Solomon, and in him was Rehoboam, and in him was Abijah, and in him was Jehosphat, and on and on, right through Uzziah, Hezekiah, Manasseh, Amon, Josiah, and Jeconiah. Down through the generations, her hope lived on, all the way through Zerubbabel, Abihud, Azor, Zadok, Eleazar, and to Jacob, who was the father of Joseph, a carpenter from Nazareth, who was the husband of Mary, who, by the way, was the mother of Jesus!

Extra, extra, read all about it! Redemption was coming through the red-light district! It was coming through Rahab the Harlot (Matt. 1:5), the woman with a past, the woman who had made one mistake after another. The woman who had messed around, slept around, and played around would turn it all around when she chose to abandon who she had been in order to become who she was meant to be. God had chosen Rahab, and she is living proof that when he chooses you, where you have been can never stop where you are going!

No doubt Rahab asked herself many questions: *How did I survive something that destroyed everyone else in Jericho? Why me? Why my family? Why did God favor us?* We have all, at one time or another, looked at our lives and asked similar questions. I know I have. Even as I've struggled to step into my calling as a pastor, a speaker, and an author, I've asked myself why God would choose me. What does he see in me? The conclusion I've come to is that God has preserved me for a purpose! He preserved me not just because of who I am, but also because of what was in me.

The reason I've survived, whenever I've found myself collapsing beneath the rubble of reproach, dying in the debris of my destructive decisions, is nothing but God's mercy. "For it is of the Lord's mercies that we are not consumed, because his compassions fail not" (Lam. 3:22). When you struggle with doubt and wonder why God has chosen you, you need to know that it's not just a random selection, some arbitrary decision on his part. He always chooses us with purpose in mind.

And he asks us to do our part, to trust him and obey his lead, to discover our own scarlet cord that we need to hang from our window. Rahab's cord foreshadows the lifeline that

God gives to each of us: the crimson blood shed by his Son on the cross. Similarly, we each discover our need for God's rescue and redemption in our lives. Often our personal scarlet cords, the things that are used to test us, become symbols of Christ's victory in our lives. And they also become a bright thread in the tapestry design God is uncovering in each of our stories.

As Rahab watched, the gold and silver, the precious stones and jewelry, the bronze and iron tools of the once-proud city of Jericho were heaped together in a special place. As the city's remains burned, she felt tears stream down her face. Grief, as well as relief, peace, and comfort from her God, flowed through her.

The valuable metals plundered from the city were now called "the treasury of the Lord" (Josh. 6:24), but Rahab knew that she, too, was part of what God had saved and redeemed from the remains of the past. She could feel it in her bones. She was no longer Rahab the Harlot. She was someone special. Rahab the Beautiful. Rahab the Rescuer. Rahab the Courageous. She would leave a legacy of faith in the Lord, not shame in the eyes of men.

As we consider what Rahab discovered inside herself, I'm compelled to tell you that you have survived all the shaky seasons of your life for a reason. The preordained purpose of God has kept you alive when everything in you wanted to die. As with Rahab, the reason we are still standing when everything around us has fallen is because of *purpose*.

He spared and salvaged us because, before the foundations of the world were laid, he made an investment. He placed his treasure in our earthen vessels. He filled us with gifts, talents, and limitless possibilities. And since he's our Creator and the only One who really knows what is in us, we have an innate need for him. We have a thirst that can only be quenched by the essence of his presence.

So like the psalmist, we are panting after him "as a deer pants for the water brook" (Ps. 42:1). He is the One our "soul follows hard after" (Ps. 63:8 AKJV), because our identity is found in him. And that is what makes a worshipper a worshipper: it is in those moments of intimate communion that he reveals to us who we are. In the heat of worship, he transfers divine intelligence into our spirits, revealing to us the mystery of his will for our lives. Little by little, he helps us to reflect on where we've been and, at the same time, unveils to us where we're going. As he does this, we start understanding that if we had not gone through what we'd gone through, we'd never be who we are. And when we understand that insight, he uses our mistakes to help us begin to help others.

Rahab was preserved, quite frankly, because she believed God. Despite her bad decisions, her careless career choice, and her seductive secrets, when God was looking throughout the city for faith, he found it in the harlot's house. Not the preacher's house, not the Sunday school teacher's house, and not even the church house. Faith had been found in a place where many would least expect it! That's because "men look on the outward appearance, but God looks on the heart" (1 Sam. 16:7 NIV). Her disappointments and her detours ultimately led her into her destiny. Because of God's purpose, what was the end for everyone else was a brand-new beginning for Rahab.

Even if you don't know your own self-worth, you have treasure inside you that is beginning to sparkle in the sun. You don't have to be a lifelong believer or sing in the choir to be chosen for God's special purposes. You don't have to have your life together and look like a perfect person. You only have to allow God into your life and let him untie the knotted scarlet cord with which you've bound your heart. He wants to rescue you because he knows what you have inside you, even if you can't see it yet. You are precious and holy in his sight!

CHAPTER THREE

I'm Not Drunk— I'm Desperate!

She didn't want him to see her cry. He had wiped away her tears so many times, had held her and comforted her, and reminded her of how much he loved her. But still something ached deep within her, a longing, a grieving for a baby she could call her very own.

It was bad enough that she had to share him with the other woman, Penny, the one who seemed to get pregnant just by looking at Elkanah. Every time Hannah glanced out of her tent, she would see the other woman glowing and smiling, rubbing her tummy where the life inside her grew. The fabric of Peninnah's garment stretched over her extended stomach and hips. And the little ones, oh, the precious boys and girls trailing behind her!

Hannah couldn't help but smile through her tears when she saw the toddlers playing in the shade of the pomegranate trees. They laughed so easily, chasing one another, and frolicking like lambs or baby goats. Sometimes, when she was younger, she would hold the babies of the older women in her village. Even then, the smell of mother's milk and the lanolin used on the infants' skin had appealed to her, the hope that someday she, too, could be a mother and hold her child to her breast.

When she had met Elkanah, she knew the Lord had been faithful and generous to her. Not only was Elkanah a good man, fair and honest in his ways and his dealings with others, but he actually loved her.

He saw something in her eyes that made him smile, and look back at her with an intensity that unsettled her in the best of ways. She gave her husband her heart as well as her body, and during the first year of their marriage, she basked in his kindness to her like a cedar in winter sunshine.

Each month she would hope and pray and ask the Lord to "let this be the one." Elkanah was quite anxious himself. Nothing would please him more than to bring a child into the world with the love of his life, Hannah. But each month, she received a reminder once again of her shame and disappointment. And their first year together had barely ended before his other wife, Peninnah, began giving her those condescending looks, those "Poor, poor, barren Hannah" looks.

It was pretty obvious that Elkanah preferred Hannah. He would return from the temple offerings and give Peninnah and her children the leftover meat. But he would give Hannah twice as much! It embarrassed her at first, but she accepted his gift just as she accepted his love. He was a good man, a kind and generous man, and she wanted to give him a son so badly. Wanted to give him living proof, flesh and blood, of the love the Lord had created between them as husband and wife. (1 Samuel 1)

WE ARE TOLD IN THE WORD OF GOD THAT "WHERE your treasure is your heart is also" (Matt. 6:21 NIV). What is the first and foremost desire of your heart today? What's the most important thing you've ever asked God to give you? Did he give it to you in the way you expected? What are you asking him to give you right now? How have you handled this kind of longing to have something special in your life? Maybe it's your college degree or a certain job in a particular line of work. Maybe it's to be married or to be a parent. Maybe it's to start your own business or to be an artist. As we get older, we tend to want bigger things—our driver's license and a car to drive, a college education (and the tuition money to pay for one), or a lavish wedding when we marry.

We all have dreams within us, and too often we feel that they're never going to happen.

It's hard to want something so badly that you ache from it. And then to watch the opportunity for it pass in front of you. Or, adding insult to injury, watching someone who doesn't appreciate it get it so easily.

HANNAH COULD SENSE THE OTHER WOMAN'S HARSH *jealousy in her withering stares. Peninnah was not only jealous about the amount of meat from the temple that her husband gave his other wife, but she knew as well that while Elkanah would take care of her and treat her well, he would never love her in the way that he loved Hannah. And she hated Hannah for it.*

One day in particular, they all went to the House of the Lord together. While Elkanah was distracted, talking with the other men, Peninnah seized the moment to insult Hannah by saying, "You may think he loves you more than me—and maybe he does, but where does he sleep when he wants a son? Whose tent does he enter when he wishes to increase the line of his family with abundance? It's a shame, really, Hannah. I'm sure you would've made a good mother. But it's clearly something that's not meant to be."

How Hannah had cried and cried in her tent after such vinegary words were poured down her throat. She simply could not understand it! She prayed and prayed and begged God. "Please, Lord," she would say, "have I done something to displease you? Please forgive my iniquity and grant me favor so that I might bear life as you have created me to do."

One night, after overhearing her pour out her pain, Elkanah came in and comforted her. "Hannah, please don't cry. I know your heart is breaking and oh, how I wish that I could fix it. You know I love you, Hannah. You mean the world to me and nothing will ever change that! Is my love for you not better than ten sons?" he would ask and smile. She would nod and let him hold her, press her damp face against the warmth of his chest and hear his heartbeat. The same even rhythm that she so desperately wanted God to ignite inside of her womb.

(Hannah's resolve only strengthened after the insults of her rival. She would not eat. She would not sleep. She would do nothing but plead before Yahweh and beg him for a child. She went to the Lord's House and prayed as fervently and as passionately as she ever had. "I will do anything for you, Lord," she cried. "Just grant *prayer* me this one thing I ask of you. If you will give me a son, I will dedicate him to you for all the days of his life. No razor will ever cut his hair and he shall be trained by the temple priests to serve you as your own. Please, oh, God! I beg you!" Like her tears, the

*words seemed to spill endlessly through her mind and heart, even as
she began whispering her desperate pleas, as if speaking them would
give them more power.*

CAN YOU RECALL A TIME IN YOUR LIFE WHEN YOU WANTED
something so badly that you were willing to humble yourself
before the Lord and beg him for it? I'm always amazed at
the number of people who tell me that they've prayed for
God to give them something and feel discouraged when they
don't get it right away. My initial question to them is, "Now,
how long have you been praying for this request? How many
times have you asked God to give this to you?" And they'll
look at me kind of funny and say, "Well, Pastor, I've only been
praying about this for a few days. I've only asked God once
or twice."

Once or twice? If someone is disappointed because they
didn't receive what they asked God to give them after only a
couple of requests, then they don't want it very much. I don't
mean to sound harsh or critical, but when I consider
someone like Hannah, as well as the many other people I
know who have prayed for years before their prayers were
answered, I have to wonder.

*   *   *

HANNAH WAS ABSOLUTELY OBSESSED WITH PESTERING God for her heart's desire. She had tried every prayer posture known to mankind. She had walked the length and the breadth of the altar, stood in place, knelt down, only to get up and stand some more. She was determined to get a hearing in the board room of heaven no matter how long it took. As the sun was going down, old Eli, the temple priest, was watching her. She had tried to ignore him, but he hovered just at the edge of her vision as she was opening and closing her eyes in prayer. He gave her a strange look, almost one of judgment and contempt, but she put him out of her mind and kept praying. The problem was, Eli couldn't hear anything she uttered because this was the silent prayer of a broken heart. Her barrenness had now become bitterness, producing a cry that was so deep she no longer had the strength to let it out.

Finally, Eli came over to her and said, "You should be ashamed! Drunk and in the Lord's House! Put away your wine, woman!"

This false accusation and unjust criticism only inflicted further pain, finally pushing her to a breaking point. Hannah looked up, her tear-filled eyes wide open. She thought, Oh, no, how could he possibly think that? *Before she realized what she was saying, she blurted out, "Oh, no, sir, I'm not drunk—I'm just desperate! I'm a woman filled with anguish and despair, crying my heart out to the Lord our God. You see, sir, I am in a situation that only God can fix. I've been asking and seeking him over this matter for a while now. I am in a season in my life where I need to find real fulfillment. Just being the baby-sitter isn't working for me anymore. I need my own now. I've been faithful over that which belongs to others and now I just need to birth my own. I'm trying to believe in God for that, but to be honest, I've very weary. Sometimes I feel so close, and then reality sets in. It seems like just when I think I can reach it, it slips right though my hands, leaving me overwhelmed. I don't mean to be out of order, or disrespectful to this temple. If it appears that way, it's because my spirit has seen something that my eyes haven't, and the most effective way I have found to bridge the gap between what I have been promised and what I actually possess is in prayer."*

The old man looked up for a moment and their eyes met. Hers wet, red-rimmed, and aching with the desire in her heart that she knew could only be relieved one way. His countenance softened and he nodded at her and said, "Peace be with you, my sister. And may the God of Israel grant you what you have asked from him."

"Oh, thank you, sir," Hannah said, with tears rolling down her face. "May I find favor in your sight." And she turned and left the temple courts knowing that there was something different about this trip to the altar. The old priest knew her plight . . . somehow he had seen into her heart and knew how desperate she was. As she wiped away the tears, she couldn't help but chuckle a bit—he had actually thought she was drunk! Wait until Elkanah heard that! Surely they would laugh together in the days to come about the priest's misperception.

Hannah was exhausted but felt at peace. It was as if her hope had taken root when she'd heard the old priest's blessing upon her. It was as if she could already sense the new life inside her that would soon burst forth.

The next day her appetite returned, and she discovered she was famished. Her energy was restored and when Peninnah sneered at her behind Elkanah's back, Hannah merely smiled and looked away. She had a secret . . . her heart's desire was about to come true. She could just feel it. Stop

HANNAH'S STORY REMAINS INCREDIBLY RELEVANT TO US as we consider our own longings and how we handle them. And it's not just because her story has a happy ending. The thing we must always remember is that Hannah was faithful in offering her heart's desire to the Lord, not knowing whether it would ever come to pass. In fact, logic and her past experiences and what seemed to be true about her body tell us she was not likely to receive what she wanted most.

The starting point for all of us with a longing is simply naming what we want. Too often, we get lost in all the busyness of coming and going and working and starting all over again; sometimes we may not even be sure of what we want. I believe this is why God gave us the Sabbath and why Jesus went away to fast in the desert for forty days. We have to get alone with ourselves and with God to know what we really want. And often we discover that what we thought we wanted is nothing more than a temporary infatuation with the things of the world.

Secondly, before we sincerely ask God to answer our prayer, we must examine our heart. Are we focused on what he wants for us and for our lives, or is this request more about how good it will make us feel or how convenient our lives will become? It's not that we can't pray for a new luxury sports car or a vacation home at the beach. The Lord can bless us in all kinds of ways, and he makes it clear that it's okay for us to ask him for anything (1 John 5:14–15). However, our motive for having that car or new home may reveal that we're not very interested in having God's will in our lives.

I'm convinced that many of the things we think we need are just temporary fickle desires so we can feel like we fit in or that we're successful. We're social creatures who are easily influenced by the people around us. Advertisers count on our ability to be molded into consumers of their products. Do we really need a new deluxe vacuum cleaner or another pair of shoes? Probably not, but if commercials can tap into our desire for a beautiful, clean home, they can sell us a vacuum. If we see how sleek and sophisticated the model who wears a particular shoe brand looks, then we might be just a teeny bit more glamorous if we have it ourselves.

And I won't even get into the ways that our family and friends influence us to be who and what they want us to be! My point is that we must begin by being brutally honest with ourselves. If all we want is a lot of money so we can idolize it, then God probably won't answer that prayer. If we are asking for money because we feel like our assignment in the Kingdom of God is to be a financial deliverer to those who are suffering from lack of provision, or trapped in poverty, then I think that is a prayer God is more likely to answer.

In some ways, the test is simple. Just ask yourself: *Is the gift that I'm asking God for just for my satisfaction? Or is it something I can pass on to someone else?* It's important to note that it's only after Hannah tells God that she's willing to dedicate her son to him that her prayer is answered.

It's not that her desire to be a mother was bad or entirely selfish, but God wants our identity to be based in him. He wants us to be who he made us to be. Sometimes when we get what we asked for—the promotion at work, the spouse of our dreams, the child we've prayed to have—we reduce ourselves to being a supervisor, a wife or husband, a mother or father, and we become solely focused on that role.

If we're asking God for something that will only

reinforce a false sense of security or identity, then it's unlikely to be answered. We must focus on following him and allowing him to use us for the unique purposes for which he made us.

WHEN ELKANAH HAD COME TO HER TENT THE NIGHT before, Hannah had prayed yet again that a new life would begin. Somehow, as crazy as it sounded, today she knew that the Lord had answered her prayers. It would be months before she would feel the tiny legs kick, the baby squirm into a new position inside her, and even more months before she would hold him in her arms. But she knew when it came to seeing her desire, it was just a matter of time.

WHAT ARE YOU WILLING TO PAY IN ORDER TO RECEIVE what you long for most? Every dream has a price of some kind, and often our patience is tested and our hearts purified by having to wait. In Hannah's story, I think it's important to acknowledge that she suffers with her desire for a child before her prayer is answered. It's not just a fleeting whim when she sees Elkanah's other wife with a baby (can you imagine!) or when she's tending the nursery at Sabbath school in the temple. It seems clear that her longing for a child goes on for some time and is something she can't let go of. The fact that she allows herself to grieve, to express sorrow and cry, seems significant.

Sometimes we work so hard to cover up these painful emotions and avoid them at all costs. Yet we need to remember that God gave us tears for a reason. They let out our sorrow, releasing some of the flood of grief that surges through us when we're waiting or hoping for something that we don't have. In my life, tears have often become prayer petitions when I couldn't find the words to accurately articulate my heart. It is good to know in times such as these that tears are the language that our heavenly Father understands.

Hannah also reminds us that suffering only lasts for a season, and that we must remain faithful even when we don't have what we long for most. We should be grateful for what we have in the midst of suffering, even when life taunts us. And it will taunt us, either intentionally or otherwise. Women who aren't able to have children will see, everywhere they look, pregnant women and babies. Veterans who have lost a limb in service to our country can't help but notice the guys out on the court playing basketball. People who have lost their jobs and can't pay their rent see their neighbor's new car, and it's like salt in a wound.

Sometimes the taunts are more direct and mean-spirited: coworkers who try to make us look bad in front of

Examples

our boss so they can get a leg up on the next promotion, women from our Bible study who use our confidential prayer requests to spread gossip, leaders who try to put us in our place by reminding us that all we will ever be capable of is following and never leading, family members who stand on the outskirts of our world plotting ways to sabotage our dreams.

The words and reactions of other people, as painful as they may be, ultimately are not what we focus on. No, we must only focus on the One who can grant us the desires of our heart. No matter how impossible our request may be in the eyes of others or how impractical it seems based on our understanding of how the world operates, we must never give up.

If you remember only one thing from the story of Hannah, I pray it's that you know you are never without hope. We may not think we have it in us, but as long as we look to the Lord, our dream has potential. Hannah sets an example for us that calls us to persevere and pester and pound on God's door until he hears our cries and grants us his blessing.

She never gave up hope no matter how desperate and hopeless she may have felt. If we bear a burden of longing for something that we believe fits within God's plan for our lives, then we must never stop asking him for it. Obviously, if it's something immoral or ungodly, he's not going to listen for long. We shouldn't be praying to find our soul mate online if we're already married! We shouldn't be expecting God to help us steal in order to launch our ministry. But if we know deep down in our heart that our request lines up with his purposes and who he calls us to be, then we must never, ever stop asking and trusting him for it.

We serve the Almighty God and for him, nothing is impossible. Even when it seems crazy to keep asking and waiting expectantly, we must persevere. Remember, people thought Hannah was drunk, yet she never allowed that to deter her from her deepest desire, and neither should you! Even when other people think we're unreasonable and unrealistic, we must never give up.

If God has laid it on our hearts, then nothing can remove it until he grants it, refuses it, or takes away our desire for it. "But Sheryl," I hear you saying, "aren't there times when we need to let go of wanting something and just get on with our lives?" Absolutely—as long as God is leading you away. We often have different desires in different circumstances and seasons of life. However, usually the kind of longings we're talking about, the "Hannah-sized" and God-designed desires for something, run deep.

And with God, all things are possible for the ones who know and serve him (Rom. 8:28). Many of us have seen or heard about people who were miraculously restored to health even when doctors said they could not be helped. We've seen people with late-stage cancer go into remission and then be declared cancer-free. We've seen homeless people start a business with change from strangers on the street. Some have witnessed couples who were told they would never have children end up having triplets. Throughout our lives, we've seen God do things that we would consider impossible if we tried to do them on our own. Never forget, when it's too much for us, it is just right for him!

Real

SHE COULD NOT BELIEVE THE WAVES OF JOY THAT WASHED over her as she held her newborn son in her arms. He was so perfect in every way. He had his father's eyes, dark and sparkling. And all that hair! His tiny fingers curled around her own as if he were holding on for dear life. The sweet smile and the soft cooing sound he made after he had nursed and his belly was full sounded like music to her ears. He was so perfect in every way. Her heart overflowed with thanks and praise to God for granting her such a beautiful, healthy baby boy.

Yes, the Lord had given her a son and she knew that from now on, there would be no more tears of sorrow and grief—she would only weep for joy. She would honor her word and would dedicate him to her most gracious God. In fact, she had named the boy "Samuel," which means "God heard me."

*   *   *

WHAT IS GOD BIRTHING IN YOU RIGHT NOW THAT requires patience and hope? What dream did he plant inside you so long ago that you'd almost given up on ever seeing it come to life? Where have you seen signs of your dream growing and building inside you?

I have to say it again: We should never, *ever* lose hope or stop asking God for our heart's desire. We should not be ashamed to be desperate in our request—even to the point of having other people think we're drunk or crazy! And from Hannah's example, we must realize that we are but stewards of all that God gives us. We must be willing to give everything back to him to use for his kingdom, including our children and the things we value most. We must keep our promises to the Lord.

It would have been so tempting for Hannah to want to hold onto her baby boy for his whole life. To make him a mama's boy and spoil him for as long as he lived. When you finally have something you want so desperately, it's tempting to cling to it. But we must remain open-handed and remember our Source, the one who answered our prayers.

We don't know we have the patience, the strength, the fortitude to wait on God's timing, but we do. When he places a desire on our hearts and we're willing to claim it with all of our being, then we must be prepared for the result. Similarly, when we discern that something we want is not from him, we must let it go as well.

Just as Hannah endured the agony of longing for a son before giving birth to Samuel, we must be willing to endure the birthing pains of the dream that God has placed in us. We may not think we have the patience to hold tight and hang on by faith. We may not know we have the energy necessary to birth the impossible, especially after we've tried so many times and failed to receive it. We may not believe that there's still time for us to bring new dreams to life. But God knows what's inside us so much better than we do ourselves. We must trust that he's bringing new fruit to life within us. We must allow our desperation to be transformed into delight! And we must never forget that prayer is the birth canal that brings to earth what God has already released for us in heaven. "What things soever ye desire when ye pray, believe that ye receive them, and ye shall have them." Whatever may be missing in your life, I dare you to pray about it, because *real prayer* is still *real powerful!*

CHAPTER FOUR

Who Do You Think You Are?

One of the current reality TV shows features corporate CEOs who go undercover within their own companies. By dressing down and wearing some kind of disguise, these bigwig executives then pretend to be new employees on the front lines of customer service and product development. They very quickly learn who's working hard and who's hardly working, who's committed to excellence and who's committed only to their own ambition. The company leaders usually learn a great deal about how their employees perceive them as well. In almost all cases, both sides have much to learn from each other. Neither is who the other thought they were.

Do you know who you really are? What's your knowledge of your true identity based on? How would the people who see you every day—your family, your boss and coworkers, your pastor and friends at church—describe you? Would they describe more than the various roles you play? Would there be themes in common, traits that demonstrate you're the same kind of person no matter where you are?

Often we don't know what God has placed inside of us because we don't know who we really are. We've accepted what we've been told, lived up to the names we've been given, and proven ourselves to be certain kinds of people. But what if that's not who we are? What if we don't know what's inside us because we haven't struggled with God to uncover our true name and deepest identity?

One of my favorite people in the Bible went face-to-face with God in a holy smackdown that resulted in the major turning point of his life. He wasn't who he thought he was. He was so much more.

It had been a long journey, and yet the hardest part was still ahead. After all of his running, all of his waiting, he finally owned more than he could've hoped for. By most of his neighbors' standards, he was a rich man, one with two wives and many sons and large flocks: goats, ewes, rams, lambs, donkeys. He had shelter and food and plenty of oil. Yet he was constantly uneasy, pacing to and from his tent to the edge of the river. Something still stirred deep within him . . . an uncertainty, yes, even a fear.

At first he thought it was just the fear he had of his twin brother, Esau. When they were young—it felt like a lifetime ago— he had ruthlessly exploited his brother and stolen Esau's birthright, their father's blessing, by lying. That their mother was complicit in helping him pull off the trick didn't help matters. He felt as if he'd been running from his brother his whole life.

When he first left home and went to live with his uncle, he had dreams in which Esau found him and pummeled his body with blow after blow. His brother was strong—as big as a grown man when they were still boys. Esau was gruff and gritty, a big hairy bear of a man, who could easily break his fair-skinned little brother's spine in two like kindling for the fire.

Would his own brother take his life the next day? Was that what he was afraid of—Esau's wrath? Jacob had listened to God about this meeting with Esau and had followed the Lord's instructions. Still . . . his brother had every right to allow his smoldering anger to ignite into an inferno. What Jacob had stolen from him could not be returned; the past could not be undone.

But this close to the unthinkable, just one sunup away from facing the bearded sneer on his brother's face, Jacob discovered that he was no longer afraid of dying at the hands of Esau. Yes, it would be harder than anything he had done so far—yes, even harder than being tricked on his wedding night the first time, forced to sleep with a woman he didn't love and then work for years so that he could marry the one he cherished. Maybe it served him right, to be tricked in return like that.

And maybe that's what this was really all about: being a deceiver, being the smooth-as-silk talker who could use words to get anything he wanted; being the smart one, the two-steps-ahead kind of guy who could lead people exactly where he wanted them to go. Lying came easily to him . . . sometimes his wife Rachel said it was easier for him to lie than to tell the truth. And what if it was? Maybe the truth needed to be framed a certain way, colored this way, shaded that way to create the desired effect.

He hated himself for it. That was his deep-hearted secret. Hated that he was always the joker, the con man, the slick pitchman, the guy grabbing his brother's heel as they came out of the womb. Jacob hated that he was always chasing after something or someone in hopes of becoming a man that he himself could respect. Always running from his brother . . . or always running from himself? (Genesis 32–33)

AFTER JACOB TRICKED HIS FATHER AND BROTHER, HE HAD to endure both solitude and obscurity in order to understand who God was and who God had created him to be. From the beginning, his life was one of conflict and confusion. Even his name meant "heel-catcher" and "supplanter," given to him because he came out of his mother's womb clutching the heel of his twin brother, Esau (Gen. 25:26).

In the Bible, name often denotes character. We don't know if Jacob was born with the personality and nature of a trickster, or if his name became a self-fulfilling prophecy. Either way, he demonstrated his character in the ways he dealt with the people and circumstances of his life.

When some people make mistakes, they spend the rest of their lives feeling like failures. I've met grandmothers who continue to feel the pain and shame of giving up their babies when they were teenagers. I've met people who were released from prison decades earlier who keep themselves behind bars emotionally. I've known recovering drug addicts who are clean and sober but can't forgive themselves for their mistakes. I've counseled people who suffered domestic abuse—both men and women—who now, years later, still feel as if they deserved it.

Just because you've made a mistake doesn't mean you can't fulfill your God-given destiny. When we ask God to forgive us and show us how to get back on the right path, he's faithful to show us his loving mercy and guide us toward our purpose (1 John 1:9). After all, we serve a God who redeems our mistakes and uses them to make us stronger, humbler, and more dependent on him.

As you rest in your God-given identity, you don't have to

base your self-worth on your own or others' false expectations or labels. You will never know what God has placed inside you if you're trying to be somebody else or you're stuck in the shame of a mistake from the past. God deposits within each of us a special purpose and set of talents with which to fulfill that purpose.

If you fight against who you really are, then you've robbed yourself of the discovery process that's part of the adventure of faith. When you're pretending to be someone other than who God created you to be, you're denying other people access to your truest self and to the divine deposit that God has placed within you to bless others.

He had been so sure that once he had his father's blessing, once he had secured what should have been his brother's, the feelings would go away. Hadn't God destined him for great things? Hadn't the Lord himself told their mother that the younger would serve the older (Gen. 25:23), that he would father an entire nation of God-fearing people?

But when stealing his brother's birthright didn't satisfy him, when remembering his old father's words—a blessing Isaac thought he was giving his favorite, Esau—only made him feel worse, Jacob ran away. He fell in love with a woman who loved him as well . . . a woman he loved enough to endure humiliation and fourteen years of hard labor as he worked for that worthless father of hers. While her love consoled him, even his beloved Rachel could not banish the accusing whispers deep inside his heart: "Coward. Weakling. Liar. Deceiver."

Jacob knew that if he didn't face his brother, he would lose all hope of ever respecting himself, ever feeling strong, like a man, not just a boy draped in adult clothes. He had sent many gifts of flocks and woven wool and oils and wine ahead to greet his brother's camp. Earlier that day, he had sent his wives and children across the river as well. He had said he needed time alone, time to pray, before seeing Esau again. But if he were honest, Jacob knew what he really needed was to see himself clearly for the first time.

HAVE YOU EVER PURSUED SOMETHING WITH ALL YOUR might and gotten it, only to discover that it didn't satisfy you? Maybe it was a promotion at work or a friendship with a certain person. It might've been a new car. It could've been membership in a country club or the inner circle at your church. You worked so hard for it and then it left you feeling just as empty as when you didn't have it.

Jacob's story reminds us about the dangers of trying to get ahead and forcing something to happen that God has not ordained as part of his plan for your life. Or equally as troublesome is trying to race ahead of God and put him on a faster timetable, as if he were a customer at a fast-food place to be rushed through the line. God will never be rushed. As the old saying goes, "He may not come when you want him, but he's always right on time."

Like Jacob conniving to steal his brother's birthright, we sometimes try to manipulate people and circumstances so that we can obtain what we think God has promised us. And he may have indeed promised us something—but he will give it to us in his time, not ours. He will open all the doors we need opened if we listen to his voice and follow him.

Throughout my life, I've never really believed that it was my job to knock on doors and then barge in before waiting on a response. I often see people strive to make their destinies happen before God has made a way for them. People think they have to have the slickest marketing tools, the right connections with people in high places, and the latest social media sites in order to get to the top. However, that's not been the case in my life. From what I've witnessed, a person's gift makes room for him or her (Prov. 18:16).

Certainly, there are times in our lives when God may lead us to approach someone and inquire about opportunities or possibilities, but we shouldn't have to push to get in. Early in my ministry, I felt God saying, "Sheryl, let me be the gentleman in your life. Allow me to open the doors for you. I'll open every door that you need to walk through. If you find yourself in front of a door that you have to push, it's not from me." I have this mental image of my heavenly Father wrapping his arm around me and reaching with his other hand to open the door in front of me. "Sheryl, if you'll let me, I'll get *every* door for you," he says as I walk through the passage he has made for me.

Rather than running off in pursuit of our own agendas, we need to find out where, why, and how God is calling us to go. If we don't, we often become confused, frantic, and exhausted by trying to do everything by our own effort. It's vital not to let yourself run ahead of God because you may miss out on his actual guidance, provision, and protection for your real purpose.

AFTER ALL SUNLIGHT HAD FADED FROM THE HORIZON, when he could no longer hear the sound of sheep and the children's voices, after darkness had descended like a shawl along the riverbank, Jacob saw a man. Or more accurately, he saw a shadow. It startled him and sent his heart racing. He looked out of his tent, and in the moonlight, with stars glistening like white sands on a blue shore, he saw the form of a man—a large man—coming toward him in a bold stride.

The embers of his fire still burned bright red and orange, so there was no doubt that the stranger saw him and his camp. At first he thought it was his brother. It would be just like Esau to sneak

away from his camp and track down his weak younger brother like
a deer in the woods. It would be just like Esau to murder Jacob
there and then brand him a coward in front of their families when
Jacob didn't show up for the big meeting the next day.

A voice inside him said, "No—that is something you *would do.*
Your brother would never think of such a devious plan." And Jacob
wept.

GOD KNEW THAT JACOB HAD A RESILIENCE AND TENACITY
inside him that Jacob himself couldn't see. Jacob had taken the
meaning of his name to heart and saw himself as second-rate,
less than his older, macho brother. Jacob thought of himself
as a con artist, a spin master, a storyteller willing to do whatever it took to get whatever he wanted. He even justified it by
assuming that God approved, since the Lord had promised
him an amazing destiny, filled with thousands of descendants.

Jacob's other strategy, running away from conflict, was
just as frustrating as trying to make things happen on his
own. He discovered that eventually he would have to face
his brother—that he needed to see him as much as, if not
more than, Esau did. And it's significant to note how their
meeting actually went the next day: "But Esau ran to meet
Jacob and embraced him; he threw his arms around his
neck and kissed him. And they wept" (Gen. 33:4 NIV). All

his fear and anxiety, a lifetime of worry and dread—all dissolved by the power of his brother's tears.

However, a large part of what made their reunion so special was the change, the internal transformation, that had occurred inside Jacob the night before he and Esau met. So much of what blocked Jacob from moving through the changes and challenges in his life was his own insecurity and misunderstanding of his true identity. In many ways, his life up to this point had only reinforced what an impatient, tricky swindler he could be. And then suddenly, he was by himself, gearing up for the big showdown with his twin brother, when a stranger showed up and started wrestling with him.

THE GROUND WAS STILL WARM FROM ABSORBING SO MUCH *sunlight, and the sand in his throat choked him with its grit. He and the stranger had been fighting—no, more like wrestling—for over an hour now. The man had not said a word but simply looked at, then grabbed him. Jacob had begun defending himself, and soon it became a battle of willpower. The stranger was clearly not his brother—he was even bigger than Esau! And strong as an ox, with hot, radiant skin like fine kid leather, smooth but with cords of muscle binding his form together.*

"Who are you? What do you want?" Jacob had repeatedly asked him. And the stranger just looked at him and started to

*smile, one of those "You know who I am" kind of smiles. Only Jacob
didn't know this man . . . did he?*

*After slamming Jacob's body to the ground for the third time,
the stranger pulled him by the hair of the head, and Jacob growled
like a wolf in anger.* Enough of this! *he thought and twisted his
way free of the other man's grasp. Jacob lunged at the stranger with
all his might only to be grabbed by the shoulders and slammed to
the ground once again. His body dripped with sweat despite the cool
winds blowing in from the desert. There was no time to think about
why this was happening or what it meant. If he wanted to stay
alive, he had to keep fighting.*

It was going to be a long night . . .

MAYBE JACOB HAD NERVOUS ENERGY TO BURN BEFORE
his big meeting with Esau, but he must've known that something strangely wonderful was taking place. He had to have
realized that this was no ordinary stranger. What was in Jacob
that allowed him to say: "I am *not* giving up! This guy is bigger than me, he's stronger than me—for all I know he may be
an angel. But I will not be overtaken without giving this fight
everything I've got, every single ounce of my energy"? And
he wrestled the messenger of the Lord all night long!

At some level, Jacob must have known that he was fighting for his true identity, his real name—Israel, a name that

means "one who has struggled with God and with man and has overcome" (Gen. 32:28). He shed the veneer of his old identity the way a snake sheds its skin. No longer would he be the trickster. Instead, he would be a strong man of God, a man of character and integrity. His heavenly Father knew these qualities were in Jacob, but God also knew he had to pierce the self-contempt and self-doubt that had become Jacob's weapons against himself.

If we're serious about discovering all that God's placed inside us, then we must not be afraid to face him with the darkest, dirtiest parts of ourselves. We need to avoid running away from painful issues in our lives and instead take our pain and shame and heartache to our Father. When we run away, we often end up more frustrated because we've basically put our life on hold until we deal with the past. We lose respect for ourselves and our confidence is shaken.

Our enemy, the accuser, berates and tempts us. Or he inflates our egos and encourages us to create a big, shiny mask to hide behind. The devil encourages us to split our integrity into pieces so that we will not be wholeheartedly focused on God. The evil one wants us to think more of ourselves, or less of ourselves, than God thinks of us. But we must remain focused on who God says we are and acknowledge him as the Source of all we are and all we have.

I travel internationally to preach. I've spoken to tens of thousands of men and women around the globe. I've been interviewed, photographed, broadcast live, videotaped, re-corded, and shown on television and heard on the radio. Pretty amazing for a girl from Detroit who failed to finish high school! Sometimes, as I'm sitting in my seat being in-troduced, I'll hear what the emcee is saying and almost forget he or she is talking about me! Then I'll pray, "God, I'm here only for you, and only because of you. If you don't go with me, then this whole event, this entire service, will be in vain. Please, Father, be with me! Make my words your words. Allow your message to come through loud and clear and help me not to get in the way."

People will ask if I still get nervous before speaking events, now that I've been doing it for a while. "Of course I do!" I always tell them. And I honestly think that's a good sign, because when you're nervous it means you have to lean on God and not on your own ability. On my own, I'll get up and embarrass myself. It doesn't matter how good I sound or how much I know. If he's not speaking through me, it's worthless. He's the reason I'm there. He's the One who called me and showed me the things inside me that I never knew were there.

IN THE EARLY MORNING HOURS, JACOB THOUGHT HE WAS having a dream. His lip was bleeding, and he could taste his own blood. His body was drenched in sweat and covered with sand and dozens of scratches and bruises. His legs hurt, his shoulders ached, and his arms screamed in pain. No matter what he did, the stranger immediately seemed to counter it. The other man seemed to absorb Jacob's blows like a sponge taking in water. But he would not give up! With tears running from his eyes and his body teetering on the brink of collapse, Jacob kept fighting.

It wasn't that he was afraid the stranger would kill him. On the contrary, the stranger could've pulled a knife or strangled him many hours ago. No, this peculiar creature seemed to be enjoying the intensity of their physical struggle. It was the way Jacob himself would enjoy a conversation with other men or the way he would relish the taste of an especially tender lamb cooked with fennel. This strange man was almost savoring their struggle.

As the first pale bands of light lifted morning's curtain in the east, Jacob sensed the man was ready to end their fight. He kept wriggling free of Jacob's grasp, trying to shake off the shorter man. But Jacob had decided that he would rather die trying to wrestle this man than live and give up the fight. He had been running and quitting his entire life. But no more. This was it.

As he held the tree-trunk-sized legs of the stranger, his adversary reached down and touched Jacob's hip. It was like lighting a fuse of pain that shattered the bone and Jacob screamed in pain. Still he would not release the stranger.

"Let go of me—it's daybreak!" said the stranger.

So he could talk after all. Why had he wrestled in silence all night then? What was this bizarre meeting all about, anyway? Perhaps it was the sunlight rising beyond them, but an idea came to light in Jacob's mind. Was it possible that this stranger was really . . . his Lord God? He shuddered at the thought and clung all the tighter to the man's thick midsection.

"I will not let go unless you give me a blessing," Jacob gasped.

The stranger suddenly stopped wrangling free and looked at him. "What is your name?" the stranger asked.

"Jacob," he panted.

The stranger helped him to his feet and held his shoulders tenderly. "You shall no longer be called Jacob. Your new name is Israel, because you have wrestled with God and with people and have overcome."

Tears streaked down his dirty, bloody face. How could this stranger have known? Surely this could only be the Lord. "Who are you?" Jacob asked, gasping for breath.

The stranger smiled and said, "Why do you ask my name?" He wrapped his arms around Jacob and put his lips to his ear and whispered his blessing. And then the stranger was gone.

Jacob fell to his knees and worshipped. "My Lord and my God!" he cried out. How long he remained there, he wasn't sure, but the sun was full above the river when he rose. As he stood, his hip continued to ache and he limped to his tent. He thought, I will call this place "sacred," for I have seen the face of God and my life has been spared.

As he bathed in the cool river and cleaned his wounds, he began *laughing and felt lighter than ever before in his life. Despite his battered body, despite the excruciating pain in his hip, Jacob—no, Israel—had struggled well and had overcome. He was stronger than he had ever realized. He didn't know such stubbornness, such power and determination, was there inside him. But God certainly knew and decided that it was time for everyone to see him as the man he was, a man with a new name, a true name. He was no longer a deceiver, but an overcomer, a fighter, a winner. He was God's beloved child.*

IF YOU WANT TO FULFILL YOUR DESTINY, IF YOU WANT TO discover your true identity and be called by your God-given name, then you must be willing to wrestle. Now, I confess, I'm not a fan of professional wrestling and probably have never watched an entire match in my life. There's something about the combination of violence and melodramatic showmanship (I'm trying to be nice!) that just doesn't appeal to me. And I'm pretty certain that when Jacob wrestled with God, it wasn't quite as over-the-top or choreographed for a viewing audience. I'm guessing there were minutes, maybe even hours, when Jacob and God were at a virtual standstill. God had Jacob pinned, and he had to keep squirming, keep trying to adjust his grip, his position, if he wanted to break free and turn the tables.

Sometimes when we feel stuck, we're really wrestling with God. During these times, we just have to hang on. I'm convinced that all of us are called to wrestle with God in order to discover our true identity. We grow up and become conditioned to think of ourselves a certain way and by doing this, we rule out other roles or attributes. I've always been a fairly quiet, reserved, some would even say shy person. I grew up the youngest child of a couple who had not planned to have more children, which explains the ten-year age difference between me and my older sister. I was the baby no one expected—not unwanted, because I was so loved by my parents, but just not what they had anticipated. They thought they were finished having children and then God said, "Surprise!" and gave them me.

Never in my wildest dreams would I have imagined that God would call me to preach. It wasn't as if I grew up as captain of the debate club or wanted to be a professional speaker someday. All during my childhood, teenage years, and many years into my marriage, most people considered me an introvert. Because I didn't like calling attention to myself, I had never developed an ability to communicate well in public.

While I didn't like to talk in front of people, my husband was a very outgoing personality and communicated very naturally and powerfully in front of others. I always joked that he talked enough for both of us and that was fine by me! We would be talking to friends or even visitors at our church, and my husband would tell a story and inevitably say, "Isn't that right, baby?" which was my cue to chime in, "That's right!" As you can see, I didn't have to say much, and I liked it that way.

Our complementary personalities held true in our ministry roles as well, and we made a great team. He was the preacher and I was the singer. My role was to prepare the hearts of the people to worship and receive God's truth while his role was to deliver that message. As far as I was concerned, that's the way it would, and should, always be. I loved God and enjoyed my role. I loved my husband (and still do!). I was a worshipper, a singer, a supportive wife and mother. Those ingredients formed the perfect portion for my plate.

Only God had more in mind for me.

He had a new name he wanted to give me. Just as I had come to accept myself as Sheryl the Shy, God thrust me to the forefront and put me in the pulpit. I suddenly found myself invited to preach at various churches with more and more frequency, and that led to being on stages and platforms that I never dreamed possible. I had no formal training other than years spent listening to other men and women of God. But something in me was soaking up everything I heard.

Of course, I had my own time spent in God's Word and discovered that the longer I knew him, the more ravenous my appetite became for his truth. And the greater my desire for other people to know him as the loving Daddy that he is. So I went from being Sheryl the Shy to being Pastor Brady! From worship singer to leader to songwriter to teacher to preacher to pastor, God has ordained my progression and opened the doors every step along the way.

Sometimes God reveals who we are gradually, step by step, before he changes our name or thrusts us into the truth of our calling. Often we must confess our false identity and hand it over to him before he can give us a new one. When God asked Jacob, "What is your name?" he was basically asking, "Who do you think you are? What is your nature, your identity?"

Jacob's wrestling with God was, in one sense, a wrestling match with himself, a struggle with his own nature. It was a process through which he had to admit who he was and confess: "Yep, I really am a trickster and a conniver." And yet there was a battle going on inside and outside that would determine his destiny.

As we deal with our own weaknesses, our own battles of the flesh, we find ourselves asking similar questions: *Why did I just do that? What's in me that made me choose that? Why am I the way I am? Why am I being pulled away from God by the desires of the flesh when what I really want is to be closer to him?*

Notice that Jacob had to fight his way into the presence of God. For the first part of his life, he was living out of who he knew himself to be. Yet this was not who he really was and did not accurately reflect God's call on his life. Once Jacob finally admitted who he had been up until that point, God reached down inside him and pulled out who he really was: Israel.

When Jacob was wrestling with God, he refused to let go until God blessed him. He refused to be so close to God, finally, and come away without the Lord's blessing. He demonstrated a longing for something more than what he'd settled for up until then. And in the process, he discovered that there was more in him than other people thought. While others saw him as a second-rate trickster, God saw him as a first-rate ruler. *Israel* literally means "he will rule as God" (Gen. 32:28). In the course of one night, Jacob went from being a court jester to being the prince destined to lead the kingdom.

When God gives you a new name, he basically tells you, "Don't accept who you are based on what other people tell you. Let me reveal your true identity to you." If Jacob had not been willing to wrestle, to get down and dirty and wallow around on the ground, to look deep within himself at who he had been and how he had acted up until this point, then he might not have fulfilled his true destiny and been an integral part of the lineage of the covenant of faith.

We are called to grab hold of God and press into him the same way. By seeking the Lord through prayer and through the Word of God, by being open to the possibility that there may be more in us than what we have seen thus far, we must challenge who we think we are in order to discover who we were meant to be. We must be willing to show up for the fight, and if we do, like Jacob we will come out of the battle with much more than we had when we went into it. It's in our painful places of life where we discover who we really are.

CHAPTER FIVE

CALLING COURAGE OUT OF A COWARD

RECENTLY I CAME ACROSS A QUOTE BY AN UNKNOWN author that said, "There are two great moments in a person's life: the first is *when* you were born, the second is when you discover *why* you were born." In my estimation, you have to live a little while before you really begin to appreciate the second part of that statement. At least that's the way it was for me.

It wasn't until I was grown with children of my own that I began wondering about the *why*s and *what*s of life. *Why am*

I here? Why was I born? What does God have in mind for me?
What am I supposed to become? What does he expect from my life?
I didn't ask those kinds of questions when I was young. I
don't think I was taught to ask those types of questions. I just
felt I had to play the hand I had been dealt, and win or lose, I
would understand it better by and by.

I never really stopped to think that maybe there was a
method to the madness of life. I think my children's generation will do better in this area because they have been exposed to the messages of destiny and purpose, and how we
have been chosen to reign in life. When I was growing up, I
heard more of an emphasis on preparing to escape life than
to take dominion in life. Most of what I was taught was about
being ready for the Lord's return.

The message of salvation, knowing Jesus as the Lord of
our lives and being ready to meet him at *all* times, was drilled
into us! We heard much about faith, healing, deliverance, and
victory, but we heard very little about how to respond to
God's expressed desires for our lives. As a matter of fact, I
didn't really think about *God's* desires for me, as much as I
thought about *my* desires for me. My prayers revolved
around his hearing me, not so much my hearing him.

In hindsight, I realize I was doing so many things backward, forging my own way, planning my own course. Then
I began hearing verses like this one from Jeremiah: "For I
know the thoughts that I think toward you, saith God,

thoughts of peace and not of evil to give you your expected end" (Jer. 29:11). I began hearing people talk about living a purpose-driven life. I started reading Scriptures that said, "Many are the plans of a man's heart, but it is the purpose of God that prevails" (Prov. 19:21). I put two and two together and through the Word, and being exposed to the ministries of so many great men and women of God, I became aware that he had already ordered my steps, and the quicker I started walking in his ways and not mine, the better off I would be.

I remember when I started hearing messages on the power of purpose. I will never forget when Romans 8:28 became real to me. All of my life I had heard the words, "All things work together for good to them that love God, to them who are the called according to his purpose." However, one day it was as if the veil had been torn and I began reading this verse in a brand-new light. I discovered that though many people quote it, especially when they are full of regret or revenge, there are prerequisites that must be acknowledged.

Yes, God promises to work all things together. *Yes*, he promises to work them together for good, but *no*, this promise is not to everyone. This promise is to a select group of people. It's exclusively to those who "love God" and to those who are "called according to his purpose." Notice this does not say "*our* purpose"!

When I realized this for the first time, I knew I needed his purpose more than anything else in my life. I knew that as much as I loved him and aimed to be like him, I was still human and capable of making mistakes. Therefore, if I was going to make them, I wanted to do so working in his purpose, so at least they could be worked together for my good. If I'm going to go through it, at least let me get something out of it!

It's not that finding God's will means we will never again do things we regret. Neither does it mean we will always make the perfect choice. Since his ways are not our ways, and his thoughts are not our thoughts (Isa. 55:8), there will continue to be times when we mess things up and miss the mark. But when you and I are in his purpose, nothing we do will go to waste. God will recycle it all together until even the bad becomes good.

This is why not knowing his purpose for our lives becomes unacceptable. It may not matter so much when we're young, but the older we get, the more we begin to understand the Scripture when it says, "Life is but a vapor" (James 4:14 NKJV). When we get a few birthdays under our belts, it starts dawning on us that time really does fly, and because it does, we must master every moment. I don't mean to alarm you, but you are not nearly as young as you think you are. If there was ever a time to seize the moment—it is now!

None of us has time to waste, and yet so many do it every day by shooting in the dark at destiny, failing to discern the difference between what *we want for us* and what *God has purposed for us*. We need to be able to honestly say to God, "As much as I want certain things, if what I'm aiming at is not for me, please tell me! Love me enough to say, 'Leave it alone!'"

We must also understand that sometimes, just because something is *not in our possession*, it doesn't mean it's *not in his will*. All the more reason we must know his will and purpose, because whatever is in his will is what he's given us divine permission to receive. My question to you is this: *What has God given you permission to possess that you don't know about yet, simply because you don't know his will?*

Who has he given you permission to become? Is there a leader inside of you that you haven't let out, because frankly, you didn't know he/she was in there? Is it time to accept that there might just be more to you than what you've thought? Could it be that you've been so content in the current stage of your life that you're about to miss out on a window of opportunity that God has ordained for you?

Are you like Gideon? Is there a great warrior inside of you despite the fact that you feel like a coward? If so, may I be the one to remind you that whenever God calls us to do something, he already knows that we have the capability of doing it? He would never ask us to do something and then fail to give us what we need to get the job done.

The very fact that he calls us is an indication that he has qualified us. He would never send his children into battle without first training them to fight. If he has called you by a new name, then let it tell you who you are, whether you feel like it or not. Name denotes nature, and when you begin to notice that God is changing your nature and character (even if only slightly), you need to acknowledge that at least the work has begun. We may not have crossed the finish line, but we are well on our way. Agree with him. Refuse to allow yourself to argue with him. If he says it's so, then it's so, because no one but God knows how to prepare us for the next step in our lives, especially when it seems beyond our own ability to imagine.

WHEAT FLOUR SIFTED THROUGH HIS FINGERS AND FELL into the basket on the floor beneath the thresher. He had hidden in the small hut used for pressing grapes into wine, hoping that none of the enemy invaders saw him enter. He should not be threshing—it was woman's work—but under the circumstances everyone pitched in so that each family, each tribe, could survive. His brothers were out hunting near the mountains to the west, but he was not strong and struggled to pull a bowstring. They made fun of him and called him names because he was so slight of build.

His father had moved their family many times during the siege from their eastern enemies. And because their tribe was the smallest and, despite his brothers' protests, the weakest, they were forced to set up camp in the least desirable spots, the rocky corner of a cave or the exposed wall of an old fortress. And as the youngest, he was always ordered around, pushed into serving instead of being served like the other men.

It had been going on for years—five, six, seven? Gideon had lost count. He couldn't remember much about the time before they were invaded. Only the hunger always gnawing inside him, the dust clinging to his robe, the smell of smoke, the sand scorched with the scarlet stain of bloodshed.

Their fields would either be destroyed just after planting season or else plundered just before harvest. The pagans took their sheep and their goats, their oxen and donkeys. They robbed them of everything valuable and left them as beggars in their own land. They mocked their God and jeered as they asked the Hebrews, "How do you like your 'promised land' now?"

GIDEON MUST HAVE HAD A REALLY HARD TIME SEEING BE-yond the tough times that were plaguing Israel. I know that when times are really hard, it can feel impossible to see the goodness of the Lord. We can't tell what God's up to or where exactly he's leading us. We want to trust him, but circumstances seem so far from what we'd hoped for that we don't know how to keep the faith.

In the book of Judges, we're told that the Hebrew people had fallen away from the Lord "once again" (Judg. 6:1), indicating the crazy roller-coaster ride that these people experienced with their faith. You would think after God sent plagues to rescue them from their captors, after he split a body of water down the middle as if it were a mud puddle, after he fed and watered and guided them through the desert, after he led them to a land of milk and honey and helped them claim it from the pagans who occupied it . . . well, you'd expect they'd be about as loyal as they could.

But they weren't. They had already struggled with constructing their own idols—a statue of a calf made from gold they melted down while they were camped in the desert. And now that they had reached Canaan, the land God promised to them, they found new pagan gods to take for a test drive: fertility gods, weather gods, and battle gods, a cultural hodgepodge they inherited from the various peoples they battled.

While it's tempting to wonder, *How could they?* based on all God had done for them, I'm convinced that we're often no different. Most of us seem to have blinders on when we're in the middle of trials or hard times. We know in our heads that God has always been faithful and provided for us. We understand that he hasn't really abandoned us, even if it feels that way sometimes. But in our hearts, we're scared and sad. We wonder if the rain will ever stop and if there will indeed be a rainbow.

SUDDENLY THE THRESHER STARTED WITH FRIGHT, KNOCK-ing over the basket of flour as he tried to stand. The small wine-press hut suddenly seemed to burst with light brighter than the sun. What was happening?

He saw a shape, larger than that of a man, and heard his voice say, "God is with you, O mighty warrior!"

This has to be a dream, *Gideon thought.* Who is this stranger talking to? *No one else was in the room, but he was the last person in all of Israel that anyone would address as a "mighty warrior." This had to be some kind of cruel joke arranged by his brothers.*

Then as his eyes adjusted to the white light, Gideon sensed the presence of the Lord and knew that this must be the Holy One's messenger, an angel sent from on high. The angel's words echoed in Gideon's head, and his temper flared. Before he could stop himself, he blurted, "If God is with us, then what are we doing here, hiding from the warriors of Midian? Where are all of his mighty miracles that brought our people out of Egypt?" He was on a roll and couldn't catch his breath. "The truth is," Gideon concluded, "our God has left us and handed us over to the Midianites."

What was he thinking? Speaking with such directness to this stranger—surely Gideon was about to die. He swallowed hard and looked at the ground. Somehow he knew that the angel was no longer before him, but God's own presence had filled the room. The voice said to him, "Go in this strength that is yours! Save Israel from Midian. Yes, you! Didn't I just send you?"

"Me, my Lord? How could I ever save my people? And with what weapon? I can't even pull the string of a bow back far enough to shoot an arrow! Look at me—I'm from the weakest clan in Israel. And I'm the runt of the litter to boot!"

Yet something inside Gideon began to stir, something that much later he would recognize as a spark of hope tindering the fire of courage inside him. (Judges 6)

ISN'T IT FUNNY THE WAY WE BEG GOD TO HELP US, AND then when he does show up, we can't believe it? Gideon was doing his job, maybe grumbling a little about the conditions he was working in, and suddenly the angel of the Lord stood next to him, saying, "God is with you, O mighty warrior!" I'll bet we could've knocked Gideon over with a feather— literally.

He tells us himself that he was the runt of the family (Judg. 6:15), probably a bit small for his age, maybe skinny and scrawny from not having fresh vegetables and enough to eat. So he can't believe that this angel has just showed up and now is addressing him—him, Gideon, of all people—as a "mighty warrior"! He basically looked up at the angel, after he found his voice, and said, "Who, me?"

So often God shows up to bless us, to guide us, to help us discover what he's placed inside us that we don't even know is there—and all we can do is stand with a blank look, asking, "Are you talking to me? I'm sorry, Lord, you have me mistaken for someone else."

It's like being in a department store or a restaurant and having another customer mistake you for an employee. They walk up to you and ask where to find the perfume counter or what the soup of the day is, and you look at them, slightly amused and just a little bit embarrassed, and say, "I'm sorry—I don't work here. I think that person over there does, though!" And you point out the real salesclerk or waitress.

That's sort of how we treat God, and how Gideon responded to the angel. *Oh, no*, Gideon thought, *there's no way anyone would ever consider me a mighty warrior.* Or a preacher. Or a teacher. Or a missionary. Or an entrepreneur. Or an artist. Or a writer. Or any of the other wonderful things that God calls us to!

Then, like Gideon, we move from the shock of disbelief and let off some anger. "Hey, wait a minute, Lord! If you've been with us the whole time, then why haven't you done something already?" And usually God reminds us, again like Gideon, that he's doing something right now—through us. But that's not what we want to hear. Because daring to believe that what God is saying about us is true requires us to let go of our fears. To release our anxieties about whether or not we have what it takes. It's hard to remain a coward when God shows up and calls out your courage.

The voice of God said, "I will be with you. Believe me, you will defeat the armies of Midian as one man."

Gideon felt dizzy and wondered if he would fall to the ground. Maybe he had been without water too long and this was a waking dream, a cruel taunt to remind him of just how weak he really was. How could he know? What should he do? Suddenly, he had an idea.

"Please—if you're really serious about what you're saying, then do me a favor. Give me a sign, something to help me know you are really from God. Stay right here and consider my humble request while I go and prepare my offering."

The voice said, "As you wish. I shall wait here."

Gideon backed out of the small hut and then ran to his home.

Women and children and a few old men watched him curiously, amazed to see him move so quickly. He had no time to talk to anyone; if this really was a message from God, he didn't want to keep the angel of the Lord waiting. (The Bible says in Judges 6:12, "And the angel of the Lord appeared unto him.")

He grabbed the storage basket of flour and threw in some water and goat's milk. He patted the dough and set it in the small fire pit to bake. Then he ran to the goat pen behind their camp and grabbed the youngest one he saw. Quickly, he killed the animal, skinned it, and prepared the meat. Never in his life had Gideon moved so fast or with such purpose.

In under an hour, he went to the sacred oak tree, the place where sacrifices were made, with his basket of meat and a container of broth, and a huge loaf of unleavened bread. There he found the angel waiting for him.

"Place the meat and bread on this rock," the angel said, "and pour the broth over it." Gideon obeyed. The angel took the stick in his hand and touched the pile of food drenched in the animal broth. Fire burst from the tip of the stick and ignited Gideon's offering!

It was true—he really was dealing with the Lord God of Israel!

THINK ABOUT HOW YOU USUALLY INTRODUCE YOURSELF at a work meeting or neighborhood party or church social event. What identifiers do you use? Identifiers are the phrases we choose to describe who we are in the context of the group we're with. If we're at the PTA meeting, we might say, "I'm Sara's mom" or "I'm Tyler's dad." When we're meeting new associates in a business setting, we might tell them, "I have a tech background and have been with the marketing team here for three years." Or even simply, "I work on Mike's team" or "I'm in HR."

Pretty soon, most of us have our little identifiers so well memorized that they roll out without our even having to think about it. Part of the reason is that we've repeated them so often, but another part is that we begin defining ourselves the same way. We start seeing ourselves as the collected collision of all the different roles we play. And that's almost always guaranteed to reduce our identities and dilute our abilities to nothing more than a handful of labels.

Gideon not only came from the least powerful, least influential tribe of Israel, but he also was its youngest member, the weakest link of the weakest chain, as it were. He obviously had become used to the role and accepted it as his lot in life. For one thing, he was threshing wheat, which wasn't exclusively a woman's job in his culture, but it wasn't something men did except by necessity. And even though his family, and his nation, lived in desperate times, it seems likely that poor little Gideon would be doing this kind of work regardless.

We see this sometimes in ourselves when we're at an

event and someone asks if we'd be willing to open in prayer. "Oh, no," we say, "I don't speak in public. But thanks for asking!" Or someone wants us to sing with the praise team or join the choir. "Nope, you've got the wrong person!" we say. Most of the time, we limit ourselves more than our abilities require us to. Why?

We're simply afraid of who we might become if we tried to stretch ourselves. If we know only how to identify ourselves as someone else's spouse, or as a parent, or as the child of our own parents, as someone's employee or somebody else's boss, then we don't have to think about who we really are. We let all those other roles fill in our job description as well as our identity.

And when God is persistent and won't leave us alone? We usually respond like Gideon: we set up a test. And if you know anything about Gideon, then you know that he was about as cautious as they come. "Are you sure you want me, Lord? Could I have some kind of sign?"

Even before we get to the fleeces for which he's so famous, Gideon tested God's initial contact with him. "Are you sure you didn't dial the wrong number?" But then when the angel lit his fire by igniting his sacrifice, Gideon realized that God doesn't dial wrong numbers.

What kind of signs do you ask God to give you? Especially in our age of constant communication and electronic information overload, it's hard for us even to hear God's voice sometimes above the clutter of all the other noise in our lives. If we're not in the habit of getting away from the clamor and listening, we may miss God's voice blessing our gifts and calling us forth to use them. Life is loud, and it is up to us to turn down the volume in preparation to hear the Voice.

Gideon took his sacrifice to a sacred place, beneath the special oak tree, to meet with God and see if this message was for real. We often have to prepare a sacrifice as well and retreat to a sacred place where we can more easily hear God. For most of us, our sacrifice is simply our time and attention, a moment of singular focus on our relationship with God. When we offer all we have and are to God, we usually discover that he's waiting to set us on fire as well. He wants to ignite our passions and stir up our longings. He knows that in every coward there's courage waiting to come out.

GIDEON TREMBLED AND FEARED FOR HIS LIFE. HE WAS dealing directly with the God of Israel! Oh, surely he would die after having seen the angel and hearing the voice of the Lord. Beneath the shade of the oak tree, despite the heat of the day, Gideon shivered and sweat rolled down his back. He was not a warrior at all. He was only Gideon, the runt, the weakling. Why did God choose him?

What could he possibly see inside Gideon that he could use to defeat the Midianites?

"Easy, now, Gideon—you surely will not die," said the voice. "Don't panic—all is well."

Gideon fell to his knees and worshipped, tears of joy and relief rolling down his face. After many minutes, as the fire of his offering burned down, he built an altar and called it "God's Peace" because the Lord had revealed himself and had comforted Gideon in the midst of his fears.

WHEN WE'RE OBEDIENT TO GOD'S CALL ON OUR LIVES, WE must often go against the grain of the culture around us. You see, obedience requires our courage and often brings the wrath of the culture around us. People have a label they've assigned to us, and when we're no longer willing to wear that label, they get upset. Suddenly we're not who they thought we were, and that unsettles them.

We often allow others to label us and then we become convinced that they know better than we do—and sometimes we believe them more than what God says about us. False labels stick to us because we allow them to. In our shame, guilt, and cowardice, we sometimes hold on to these labels, as painful as they are, rather than risk hoping that we could be more. But God delights in forgiving, cleansing, healing, and restoring us. The Bible tells us that we are no longer who we used to be since we have been made new creatures in Christ (2 Cor. 5:17).

Like Gideon, we can create new names for ourselves and change the way people see us. Gideon eventually became known as "Jerub-Baal," which means "let Baal fight his own battles," because he toppled his father's idols to this pagan god. His new name seems fitting, since the name Gideon itself means "warrior" or "one who causes others to fall in battle" (Judg. 6:32).

I shared with you earlier how difficult it was for me to dare to believe that God was calling me to preach. I'll never forget the first time I had someone call me "Pastor Brady"! It took me a minute to realize they were talking to me!

THAT VERY SAME NIGHT, AFTER HIS ENCOUNTER WITH the angel, Gideon received a Word from the Lord. God told him to take his father's best bull, one in his prime, destroy the altars to false idols that his father had built, and sacrifice the bull there on a new altar to God. Gideon knew he would need help and the cover of darkness to pull off such a feat. So after nightfall, he got ten servants to help and did as God had instructed.

Just as he expected, the next day, their entire community was up in arms. "Who did this?" they demanded. Joash, Gideon's fa-

ther, stood up for his son, maybe even with a hint of admiration. Maybe Joash didn't know Gideon had it in him to make such a bold move, but now that it was done, his father appreciated him for it. Gideon liked the way that felt.

Joash told the objectors that if Baal was really a god, if he had any supernatural power at all, then Baal didn't need the men to stand up for him. Even though Joash apparently had these altars to false idols himself, he was only trying to fit in with his neighbors. He knew down deep that they had no power and could not compare with the one God of Israel.

So the pagan gods were overturned by Gideon's boldness, and everyone, including his own family, realized that they were mistaken about labeling this little guy who had become the warrior of the Lord.

WHEN GOD CALLS US TO USE WHAT HE'S PLACED INSIDE us, we must expect that we will discover new qualities inside ourselves, especially the courage to be our true selves. People may be surprised because of what they've come to expect from us. Yet when we're empowered and unleashed, they're often forced to see us in a new light. Similarly, we must get used to seeing ourselves differently, and it's not always easy.

Many people who lose significant amounts of weight struggle to see themselves accurately at their new lighter weights. They're so used to viewing themselves as heavy and beating themselves up because of their struggles with food that even when they're eating healthfully and look dramatically different, they still can't accept their new selves. But the scales don't lie, and neither does God.

When he calls us to do something, to unleash all that he's placed within us, then we must act in obedience, even when we don't see what he sees. We don't have to see ourselves as mighty warriors to act like them. This is not trying to "fake it till you make it," but rather "faith it till you make it." If God says that we're warriors (or preachers, artists, teachers, or doctors), then we can trust that this is true despite our insecurities and past experiences.

GIDEON DID NOT RECOGNIZE HIMSELF AS HE LOOKED IN *the clear pool of water. The man he saw was bearded and weary, with a fire in his eyes and the heart of a warrior beating in his chest. He laughed to himself. Yes, God knew there was this deep part of him that he never would have discovered if the Lord hadn't called it out of him. He touched the hilt of his sword and smiled once again.*

* * *

As we've seen consistently in our other chapters, God often chooses the least likely candidates (from our earthly point of view) to do his work and fight for his kingdom. Whom does he choose to help his spies take over the city? A prostitute named Rahab. Whom does he use to save the life of one of the most powerful generals in the ancient world? A maid whose name we don't even know. Whom does he choose to bless with a son as the answer to her deepest longing? A woman named Hannah who prayed so desperately that others thought she was drunk.

And whom did God choose to defeat the Midianites and save the nation of Israel? A ninety-eight-pound weakling named Gideon, who second-guessed and continually tested God each step of the way. Notice that even after Gideon's name had been changed for successfully toppling the idols, he still couldn't accept the fact that he was the one God had chosen. It's as if he simply didn't have the capacity for viewing himself as a leader, as the man God wanted to use to destroy their enemy's army of over one hundred thousand men. After he had gathered together an army of men to stand against the Midianites, Gideon threw down the fleece just to be really, really, really sure that God wanted him to lead the charge (Judg. 6:36–40).

Gideon may have been afraid—of dying in battle, of looking silly, of not being a good leader. After all, he'd been told his entire life that he was a weakling, not a warrior. Another motive may have been to build his confidence before the big battle. Maybe the memory of the angel's visit had begun to fade. Maybe Gideon had started to believe that he'd dreamed up the whole thing.

The sign he asked God to display is almost comical. The first time it was to make the fleece wet and keep the ground dry. The next night it was to keep the fleece dry and make the ground wet. And both times, God did as Gideon requested, and made it 100 percent crystal clear that he was indeed God's chosen leader, a mighty warrior who would save his nation.

Often God inspires us to be shrewd and strategic, resourceful and innovative, in order to accomplish his goals. Force and might are not what ultimately win our battles. When we rely on God, we know who we are because he has called and convinced us. We know that he's a God through whom all things are possible, even using someone like us for mighty deeds. Even calling courage out of a coward and transforming him into a warrior.

He continues to call courage out of us today, piercing our fears and insecurities, peeling away the labels that others have stuck on us, and showing us who we really are. And when we know who we are, and whose we are, we will always find a way to win the battle.

We are overcomers. We may have to keep our torches hidden for a while until God tells us the time is right. But then, we must let the world see our light and not be afraid to give all we've got to the fight. God is with us!

Isn't it time you unleashed the warrior that's inside you? You may be weary or weak, tired or timid, but God knows that you have the power within you to fight his battles. When he calls you to fight, you don't have to be afraid or ask for proof. You may not see what's inside you, but your courage and strength and power are there because God put them there. Let your warrior loose!

CHAPTER SIX

FINDING FAITH
TO FLOAT

I HAVE TO CONFESS: I DON'T LIKE TO WATCH THINGS
crash or sink, especially if it's a vehicle or machine I have to
use regularly. Needless to say, I've never seen the movie *Ti-
tanic*! And that first episode of the popular TV series *Lost*—
you know, where the 757 Airbus crashes on some deserted
island? Not a chance! Recently I was flipping channels after
talking to my sister and came upon another movie about a
plane crashing. Flying is too much a part of my life for me to
watch a movie like that!

Still, I've sat next to people who can watch a movie at thirty thousand feet about a plane crash while sipping a cocktail and being totally entertained. It doesn't faze them! But I couldn't watch one of those shows if I was on dry land and knew I'd never fly again. I don't want those images running through my mind.

While I like cruises, I must admit that the tragic sinking of that enormous Italian cruise ship gave me pause. It just goes to show that nothing and no one is invincible. I remember when I took my first cruise, I was amazed at the size of the ship, how something so big and heavy could still float. I was also mesmerized by the layout of that ship because ever since I was a little girl, I'd wondered what the very first cruise ship—Noah's ark—must've been like.

Whenever I heard the story of Noah, my mind instantly filled with questions. Were there rooms inside the ark, or just one big cabin? Surely, each of the pairs of animals needed its own stall, right? How did Noah's family know where they were going? Or did it matter, since the whole earth was covered with water? Did they ever lose hope that the rain would stop and the floodwaters recede?

As I grew older, there was one more question that has always lingered in my mind: What was Mrs. Noah like? Was she totally committed to the vision of her husband? Did she have secret questions about the validity of his assignment from God? Did she question his skill set, his ability to build such a massive structure? (Such a structure had never been built before in the history of the world.) I'm sure Noah had a lot of talents, but prior to this story, I don't recall anything showing up in Genesis about him being a shipbuilder. Did Mrs. Noah ever wonder what she'd gotten herself into? I suspect that she struggled with all of these challenges and more, just as you or I would.

IMAGINE THAT THE PERSON YOU LOVED MOST RECEIVED A clear and direct message from God. And obeying God's instruction meant that your spouse must begin a project that made no sense whatsoever. It wasn't just unusual—it was outright crazy! And yet you'd never seen your spouse more confident about what it meant to obey the Lord.

But here's the thing: God told your husband to build a boat—a really, really big one—but you didn't live anywhere near the sea! We're not talking a little fishing boat, a kayak, or a canoe. This wasn't Huck Finn's river raft or even an elegant sailboat. Your family lived in a dry, arid, Middle Eastern climate, with the nearest body of water many miles away. But God had told your husband to work on something no one had seen before—an ark—a boat far larger than the house in which you lived. So he started building this new thing. In your backyard.

And you wanted to be supportive, you really did. You loved this man: he was an amazing father to your three sons. Even if the town had abandoned the old ways of worshipping the Lord their Creator, and turned instead to all kinds of wicked pleasures, most people knew that your husband still actively prayed to Jehovah and lived out his beliefs. He treated others fairly and kindly. He gave food and clothing and shelter to those in need. He prayed every day and faithfully obeyed all that God asked of him.

Which had been fine up until recently . . . He spent days into weeks cutting cypress trees, lifting and cutting and straining and struggling; he worked every day in the extreme heat. And he wasn't a young man anymore—well over five hundred on his last birthday—and only occasionally allowed your sons to help. Your sons didn't know what to make of their father's behavior and this enormous ship any more than you did. But you trusted him . . . what else could you do? You prayed to God and asked for his instructions, and all you received was a sense that you should support your husband's obedience.

After many weeks, the huge ark began to take shape. The people around you laughed and mocked your husband. They made gestures and rolled their eyes and pointed him out to each other. He would warn them, of course, tell them that they needed to give up their worldly pleasures and seek the Lord God of creation. Some listened and openly scoffed, while others seemed troubled by your husband's words. But even when he was warning them, he kept on cutting those enormous planks of cypress wood. Even when he was in your tent after the evening meal, he *would sit and whittle the thick pegs that he used to nail the boards together.*

Soon he took a large metal tub and placed it over the fire and began making a thick, dark pitch that he used to seal the cracks between the planks. You asked him how he knew how to do all this— it's not as if he sailed the seas before he started this new project. He said God told him exactly how to make it, down to measurements and building materials.

People would ask, "What are you building, old man?" and he would just smile and say, "An ark." And they would roar with laughter. He would just smile sadly and say a prayer for them. (Genesis 6–8)

HAVE YOU EVER HAD AN "ASSIGNMENT" SO DIVINELY IN-spired, so God-ordained, that you couldn't think about anything else? It may have expressed itself as part of your dream, your heart's desire. Maybe it was having your own home, or getting out of debt. Or maybe you always dreamed of having your own business, a company unlike any other you'd ever seen. Maybe it was creating a mural or writing a book. Maybe it was raising a God-honoring, Lord-loving family.

Or, like Noah, maybe your assignment from God was something you didn't understand at first. It may seem mysterious and even crazy, something that others don't understand or grasp—and you don't know how to explain it to them other than to make it clear that you must obey God's directions.

Noah must have felt this way. He worked months of hard labor to bring about his vision, the blueprint for saving himself and his family. Where you or I would make a trip to the Home Depot or Lowe's for the supplies we need, Noah had to make everything himself—the saws, the nails and pegs, the hinges, the doorknobs, the windows, and gates for the animals' stalls. His dream demanded a dedication to details.

But from his point of view, Noah had no choice. His assignment was clearly given by God, so it was a matter of trust and obedience. Everyone around him was going in the opposite direction, chasing after sensual gratification and worldly pleasures. They didn't understand what this strange old man was doing and couldn't believe that it even mattered. Surely he was out of touch, living in the past with his prayers and his God and his warnings, right?

Wrong. Noah was told to build something that the world had never seen before. He probably didn't expect other people, at least those outside his family, to understand what he was doing. He could only hope and pray that they would listen to the message God had given him and change their ways. But through it all, Noah knew he could not let anything stop him. It didn't matter how weird other people thought he was. It didn't matter that he didn't live next to the sea or that no one had ever done what he was being called to do.

It was simply a matter of obedience to his God. Noah knew the Lord so intimately, walked with him so closely, that he didn't have to think twice about what God asked him to do. In those hundreds of years he lived (we're told Noah was six hundred years old when the earth flooded!), he had learned that God's ways are not man's ways. He had grown and matured in his faith so that he could discern God's will and just do it.

In our culture today, it's rare for most people to obey authority figures blindly. Maybe it's because we've seen so many leaders abuse power and deceive their followers, those they were supposed to be serving. Maybe it's because we're used to the media putting a spin on everything so that we never can trust that we're getting the full story. Maybe it's because we don't like having other people tell us what to think. But for whatever reason, I'm inclined to think that blind obedience no longer exists.

And maybe this is a good thing. Certainly, people are only human and do indeed abuse their power and need to have accountability. But there's one relationship that requires, not blind obedience, but what I like to call God-vision—the ability to focus on God's leading and to follow him. Noah had God-vision and knew that just because he had never built a boat before didn't mean he couldn't build one. He knew that just because rain had never fallen before didn't mean it wouldn't. He knew that just because people made fun of him didn't mean they were right. Ultimately Noah knew that just because something seems impossible for a person to do doesn't mean it's impossible for God to do.

Noah heard God's call on his life and answered it without hesitation. He set to work and started cutting the wood, sawing the planks, making the pitch, measuring the dimensions. He built it a board at a time, plank by plank, level by level, until he had constructed a boat every bit as big as that cruise ship I was on. He was faithful in assembling the small pieces necessary for building a big boat.

What is God calling you to accomplish in your life? What unique structure, something so special and fresh that nothing like it has been seen before, is waiting for you to build it? What pieces should you be assembling in your life right now in order to construct your ark board by board?

So often we hear God's voice directing us and then feel overwhelmed by what he's asking us to construct. "An ark? Me?" we say to him. "Oh, Lord, I'm flattered that you would ask, but you know I'm no good with a hammer—and I can't even swim!" We come up with excuses and indicate why we can't do something instead of demonstrating Noah-style faith, a faith that floats. Creating an ark feels too big to us, so we remain overwhelmed by the sheer size and scope of what

God calls us to build, instead of breaking it down into a step-by-step process.

We think that just because something hasn't been done before, we can't possibly do it. We're not making excuses based on our identities but on our abilities, or lack thereof. We forget that God always gives us directions and instructions for building new things. We forget, as Jesus told us, "With man this is impossible, but with God all things are possible" (Matt. 19:26). He knows what we're capable of so much better than we do. Too often, we limit ourselves because we're unwilling to take a risk. Or else we take a risk and then refuse to keep going.

Any inventor, any innovator, any ark-builder knows that you must learn from the things that seem like mistakes or failures and risk again. Thomas Edison made hundreds of attempts to get an electric lightbulb to work before it actually lit up in front of him. What if he had stopped after only one try, or after only a dozen tries? I'm convinced that when we trust God, he will use everything in our lives to equip us. We obey him and demonstrate that our faith floats. We might go under the water a few times, but our faith always rises back to the top.

THE ARK WAS FINALLY COMPLETED, LOOMING LARGER than anything you'd ever seen. And larger than anything your neighbors had ever seen. They laughed at the enormity of it and made jeering sounds as you and your family gathered up the pairs of animals that God had asked you to bring on board. Any doubts you had faded a long time ago and you knew God had spoken, and your husband obeyed, so that your family might be saved. You began try-ing to warn people as well, but no one would listen. All they would do was laugh.

But no one was laughing when the rains started. The first day brought cause for celebration, an end to the near-drought conditions that had left the ground dry and barren. The second as well. But by the third day, the water stood ankle-deep along the footpaths and narrow roads. Streams formed along ditches and gullies and pushed across the land with the force of a mighty wind. And still the rains continued. Great sheets of fat, wet drops were falling like a gray curtain from the sky.

Finally your husband told you it was time. "Call our sons and their wives," he said. "And just as important, make sure all the animals are on board and sorted." Seven pairs of some, male and female, only one pair of others. You could not believe that all of those creatures were going on this boat with you. But when you saw the inside, all of the rooms and compartments, all of the stalls and decks, you knew that God had guided your husband. It was orga-nized far more thoughtfully than you knew he could have come up with on his own.

The rains fell day and night, day and night, for what seemed like years but was actually only forty days and nights. It was even hard to tell the day from the night, with the angry, gray clouds giving way to darkness only to lighten slightly when day returned. And water all around you on every horizon!

The floodwaters had quickly swallowed everything around you, had washed over houses and tents and huts, animals on hillsides, people in the streets, birds in the trees. The screams and cries of so many people were swallowed up by the rushing current. Like a mighty ocean returning to high tide and washing away everything in its path, so this flood from heaven purged the earth.

WHEN GOD REVEALS HIS WILL WE MUST, AS NOAH DID, obey without worrying about what others think. It's human nature to want to fit in and be part of the group, to do what everybody else is doing. I can remember feeling this way so strongly when I was a teenager. If all the other girls had white boots, then I wanted some just like theirs. If the cool thing was to wear just a little bit of lipstick, then I wanted to stop at the drugstore and pick out a shade.

And I'm sure my mother said to me the same thing that I later told my children when they asked to do something I didn't think safe or wise. "Well, everyone else gets to go," they'd say. To which every parent knows the response: "If everyone else jumped off a cliff, would you?"

As we get older, we sometimes think that we're beyond

peer pressure, that we're stronger and more independent than any need to fit in with those around us. But if we're honest, most of us want to belong somewhere, want to be accepted and respected, admired and appreciated by others like us. Even in Christian circles, we end up reading the same books and listening to the same music just because everyone at our church is doing it. Sometimes we even let others shape our beliefs rather than looking firsthand at what God says.

The reality Noah experienced in his culture is the same for us today. So many people around us won't understand our faith and won't even want to try. They will dismiss us as crazy or fanatical or make fun of us for obeying the call of God on our lives. They will rely on what they can see and touch and be skeptical of anything divine or Spirit-led. Sometimes these individuals may even be people close to us; our own family members may not understand our faith.

I'm convinced that at some points in our lives, others will consider us foolish when they see us obeying God and building something new. Noah was willing to let others think him a fool, even as he tried to warn them and tell them the truth. He didn't become smug and self-righteous with a better-than-thou attitude. I believe he genuinely wanted other people to change their ways and allow God to save them. But no one did. The Bible says that they had given up on God, and because of their abandoned faith, God was grieved and wanted to purge the earth and start over.

Noah, however, was the exception. He was the one honorable, God-fearing man left on the earth. God knew that he could not destroy Noah with the disobedient and instead used Noah's faith to repopulate the earth. Noah allowed himself to be God's chosen vessel for a fresh start, a new beginning.

Where is God calling you to take a stand in your life, even if others ridicule you? Are you willing to obey your Father's voice even when it doesn't seem logical or even rational? Now certainly, God never calls us to do something that violates his own character and principles. He's not going to lead us to harm others or ourselves. He will not lead us to sin, but he often asks us to trust him beyond what we can see. Just like Noah. And just like so many other pioneers of the faith that we're exploring in this book: Ruth and Naomi, Gideon, David, Rahab, and Hannah.

If we want to discover all that God has placed inside us, then we must be willing to step out in faith. We must be willing to build the arks God calls us to build. We must be faithful in the small things in order to accomplish the enormous structures that wait ahead for us. We must be willing to cultivate the new seeds he plants in us in order to yield a new harvest in a new season. We must not be afraid to take a stand for what is right amid a culture that's committed to selfish excess and immediate gratification.

FINALLY, THE RAINS STOPPED AND THE SKY EVEN SEEMED to brighten a little, pale and luminous. You and your family had never seen so much water in your life and you longed to sight even the smallest scrap of land, the faintest branch of a tree, the palest green of a leaf. But for dozens of days, you could see only the churning waters, blue and green and gray, for as far as your eyes could see. No land, no people, only water.

When the sun at last came out again, you and your family stood on the upper deck of the ark and wept and laughed together. Your provisions had held out, although the living conditions made you feel more and more claustrophobic. And you were so tired of the work required to keep the animals healthy. The smells, the chores of cleaning their stalls and pens, of feeding them, allowing them time to run or gallop along the top decks—it was exhausting.

Then one day, your husband sent out a dove, in a great swoosh of white feathers and flapping wings. The sight of the bird made you hopeful and a bit sad at the same time. Then the joy you felt when the dove returned with a green olive branch in its beak! Your sons and their wives laughed and shrieked in celebration and your husband smiled because soon you would be on land again.

And sure enough, within only a few days you spotted land—mountain peaks and the tops of trees. The floodwaters were receding. The sun was bearing down and bringing new life and drying up the drenched earth. Then one day, a great mountaintop ahead, a place called Ararat, loomed and the ark stopped. Your feet touched the muddy earth for the first time in months and you couldn't help but bow down and worship, grateful that you had been spared, thankful to be on land again.

God promised that he would not flood the earth again, and as a sign, he showed you something else you'd never seen before: an amazing arc of colored lights—red, orange, yellow, green, blue—reaching across the sky like a beautiful bridge. Your family called it a "rainbow," since it reminded them of a hunter's bow. You knew that this colorful arc would serve as a reminder of God's covenant, his promise, to preserve his people and restore the earth. It was the most beautiful thing you'd ever seen.

SOMETIMES EVEN AFTER WE'VE COMPLETED THE ASSIGN-ment God has given us, we must remain patient. We still have to work hard and remain obedient as we wait for our next assignment. We can't just rest on our big accomplishment as the pinnacle of our lives. Sometimes we have to ride out the storm, perhaps even realizing that what God has called us to build is the means of our survival.

When I moved my family and ministry from Raleigh, where we'd been for ten years, to Dallas, it was a huge undertaking and sometimes felt as if I were trying to turn around Noah's ark! So much energy and effort, time and hard work went into all the details of the move. For months and months, all our attention was focused on getting from Point A to Point B.

Once we were on the other side of the move, part of me wanted to just take a few weeks (or months!) off and recover from the exhaustion of the transition. And while I certainly rested and recovered, I realized that I had just boarded the ark that God had been helping me create my entire lifetime. In some ways, the new season had just begun, and it was time to get busy looking ahead, anticipating dry land and the new growth that would follow. It was time to look for the rainbow and remember his promise to me. My faith had been tested, and even though my burdens sometimes felt as heavy as one of those cruise ships, it also floated like one of them.

Certainly for Noah, his faith floated as the ark sustained not only his own life but also that of his household, as well as representatives from the entire animal kingdom. It's important to note that Noah was successful in doing what God called him to do and was blessed for it. His job was not to go around trying to rescue people from the floodwaters. No, he was called to warn people and to build the ark. He was called to sustain life and to be the vessel for God's re-creation of the earth. Noah was elevated for his faithfulness, and the impact of his obedience saved his family as well.

Often when we're in the midst of difficult circumstances, we can't see what God is doing or how he is using us. But if we're living in faith and obeying his Word, we can trust that he is using us to bring about new life. How can you see his hand in your life right now? What example are you setting for those in your own household? Is your family closer to God, protected from the floodwaters of our culture, because of your faithfulness?

Noah had no idea that God would use his actions as a life preserver. You and I are here today because of his faithfulness and obedience. He reminds us that we all have choices about how we will respond to God's voice. We can ignore his calling or even angrily refuse to obey, as Job's wife did when she cursed God and suffered her own destruction as a result (Job 2:9). Or we can be a lifeboat on the seas of life, just like Noah.

I challenge you to consider what God is calling you to build in your life and how it can be used to bless others. If you're going through a trial or weighed down by a heavy burden, I encourage you to consider how God is providing for you and to remain faithful. He has never failed you and he never will.

Maybe like Noah, you're in a tight place. Possibly you feel restricted and limited. You can't move the way you used to move, or do what you used to do. Maybe you're in a stinky place, wondering if the God who shut you in it has forgotten where you are. Perhaps it feels as if the storm is never going to stop.

Wherever you are and whatever you are facing, never lose hope for the rainbow when the rains are falling. There was more to Noah than meets the eye, and the same is true for us when we're willing to obey God, when we're willing to have a faith that floats.

CHAPTER SEVEN

MORE THAN A MAID

D O YOU EVER FEEL AS IF WHAT YOU DO EACH DAY doesn't really matter? Whether it's staying at home with the kids or calling on new accounts, babysitting or acquiring a multimillion-dollar business merger, at some time or another most people begin to wonder if what they do makes any difference in the world. Maybe we know it matters, but it's just hard to keep our worth in mind as we answer e-mails, return phone calls, pay bills, change diapers, and do chores around the house.

On the other end of the spectrum, have you ever met someone who thought too highly of him- or herself? Someone who demanded star treatment? Have you ever met someone famous who seemed to have an air of entitlement? I've been privileged to meet some unique dignitaries through my ministry, and what I've discovered is that really successful people are usually down-to-earth, humble, and respectful. On the other hand, I've met a few people on their way up who acted as if they were entitled to have the world bow at their feet.

You know the kind—the impeccably groomed man in the dark suit demanding the best table in the restaurant. The beautiful young woman in designer clothes who refuses to speak to the housekeeping staff at the hotel. The meeting manager who bullies others in the boardroom. The person who cuts in line in front of you at the airport. The person who brushes past you in the department store.

I'm guessing most of us would never identify ourselves as that person, but I'm convinced we all act entitled sometimes. Just as we often fail to realize that what we do each day matters, we often try to make the world bend to our will. In either case, the cause is the same. Whether we're thinking too highly of ourselves or not highly enough, the problem stems from misplacing our identity. Instead of celebrating the unique and wonderful people God created us to be, we tend to focus on what the world tells us to look at—externals, titles, money, success, fame.

All of us are tempted to place our identity in things—I call them "stage props"—instead of realizing who we are as God's children. Maybe it's the title on our business card or the size of our corner office. Maybe it's the part of town we live in. It could be the school our kids attend or the church where we worship. And, of course, there are always the stage props of success: designer clothes, luxury cars, beautiful shoes, and the latest tech gadgets.

It's amazing how certain accomplishments can cause us to have a certain sense of self-importance. However, sometimes the most important people are the ones who don't get the credit. The people who serve behind the scenes or quietly lead without fanfare. The people who treat everyone the same regardless of what they're wearing or their net worth. Sometimes we are these people, on the opposite end of the spectrum from those at the top. We may feel insignificant, underappreciated, and overlooked. But everything we do matters, and sometimes God uses a small hinge to open an enormous door.

THE SCREAMS GREW LOUDER AND THE SOUND OF HEAVY footsteps thundered through the night. Strange voices and the clattering of swords. The world as she knew it was turned upside down. Was she dreaming? The smell of scorched earth and woodsmoke as-

saulted her as she bolted awake and immediately called out to her family. "Mother? Father? Are you there? Where are the little ones? What is happening to us?" she called out.

She heard no response as she frantically ran from small room to small room in search of her family. Their door had been reduced to kindling and the table upon which they ate their meals had been overturned. Her gut clenched and she feared she would be sick. She prayed to Yahweh for the safety of her family and for this nightmare to end.

Quickly looking out the window, she thought she saw her mother being dragged behind a giant-looking soldier. "Mother!" she choked and began to sob. Someone heard her cry and before she realized it, she, too, had been captured and was being pulled along by calloused hands. She trembled, knowing her life would never be the same. (2 Kings 5)

SO OFTEN WHEN WE FIND OURSELVES THRUST INTO A trial and our lives start falling apart around us, we struggle to see how it can be part of God's plan for our lives. When all we're experiencing is loss and all we're feeling is grief and anger, it can be hard to trust God. When our world is rocked by disaster and devastation, by calamity and crisis, we can't usually see what God is up to and where's he's taking us. We feel as if we don't have the strength to get through the pain, let alone to ever experience joy and peace again.

For years, I taught on the biblical character Naaman, thinking that obviously he was the star of the show. After all, he's the military hero who faced a battle that no man could win—leprosy. But the more I've reflected on and researched this story, the more I'm convinced that the central character is a young girl—we don't even know her name—who had been taken captive during the many battles between Aram and Israel.

Naaman's maid was a small hinge that swung a big door.

This little girl, taken as a spoil of war, impacted a mighty general, the king of Syria, and even the prophet Elisha. Ripped from what she had always known, this young woman was bound and forced to go with the brutal soldiers who had destroyed her village and ravaged her house. Forcibly abducted from a godly Hebrew home, and one that honored the man of God, Elisha, she was dragged into a heathen land, Aram (which we now know as Syria), where the people worshipped many false gods.

This one young woman—all the idolatry she had to witness, all the losses heaped on her heart—it's hard for us to imagine. Somehow she would have to endure and hold on to her faith. Perhaps she was mocked for her beliefs, ridiculed for trusting in the God of Israel, who had apparently allowed her homeland to be conquered and she herself to be enslaved.

What is pulling you away from where you want to be right now? What false idols are blocking the path for you to discover all that God has placed inside you? Are you stuck in the losses of the past, still mourning all that used to be, or have you caught a glimpse of God's goodness and continued to trust him despite your hard circumstances?

Naaman's maid could have been angry and antagonistic. No one would blame her for resenting the situation thrust upon her. She could have pouted and connived ways to escape or to harm her new master, Naaman. Instead she built up her faith, and it became contagious, ultimately allowing her to win her mistress's trust and her master's miracle.

And they clearly had a relationship, because she was not afraid to talk about Jehovah, her homeland, her faith, and the man back in Israel with the power to heal her master's condition. She displayed true courage, grace under pressure, and she gained the respect of her master and his wife. They listened to her and heard the sincere concern and hope in what she proposed.

After all she'd been through, it's pretty amazing she had any hope left, let alone had enough to share. Something in her just kept on giving and giving and giving. And the more she gave, the more she had to give. Whatever she'd been through was obviously not enough to shake the core of who she was and what she had in God.

Before she was captured, she had no idea of the strength of her resolve. She had no idea how great God was inside of her. She was clueless as to how big her future was. She never would've imagined that all these years and generations later, we would still be talking about *her* story. To many she was a mere maid. A part of the landscape around her master's mansion. Just a faceless, nameless, powerless young woman.

Yet despite all the loss in her life she remained true to herself, to her integrity and personal dignity. She remained faithful to her God, even in the midst of slavery and exile from her home. She didn't become a victim and abandon her faith. She clung to it and God became her lifeline.

God had a plan for her despite the brutal circumstances she had to survive to even become a part of Naaman's life. She certainly didn't understand why she was there, but God did. She didn't know she could help him, but God did. She'd never gone to medical school, but she talked him straight into a life-preserving miracle.

As she finished making the bed, she couldn't help but hear the groans of pain coming from her master's chamber. For many days now, she had noticed how sick her master had become, how weak and feeble, how downcast in spirit. She prayed for him, prayed that the Lord her God would heal this man who should have been her enemy. She trusted God too much to hate and she knew that Naaman wasn't a bad man; he just didn't know her God. At least—not yet.

Later, while she was folding clothes that had dried in the sun, she saw an opportunity and took it. Her master's wife was arranging flowers and herbs in a basket.

She spoke with a mixture of urgency and respect to her position: "My master is so sick—we have to do something! I know there's no cure . . . but I know a prophet, a holy man back in my country. He knows God and can do powerful things. He can heal sick people."

The older woman looked at her and offered a sad smile. And then something shifted in her eyes. They were desperate—why not hear what this little slave girl had to say? What else could they do?

HAVE YOU EVER FELT AS IF GOD WAS CALLING YOU TO reach above your station in life and offer life to those above you? It can feel scary, crazy even, to think that the people who are our bosses and pastors and leaders actually need us to help them. But they do. We all need each other in ways that defy our job descriptions and tax brackets. Naaman's maid could have kept silent—she could even have enjoyed a kind of revenge by remaining silent.

She might have thought, *I know Elisha, the prophet, could help my master, but why should I try to help him? Isn't he responsible for my family being destroyed and my life becoming a nightmare? If it weren't for him, I wouldn't be a maid. If he's going to treat me like a servant, then I'll just act like one and keep my mouth shut!*

But this young woman could see beyond her past losses and present imprisonment. Greater still, she could see that God was still in control of all three—her past, present, and future. Her faith sustained her, even though she couldn't understand why he would allow what had transpired in her life.

When this young girl joined their household, Naaman and his wife had no idea that he would get leprosy and face a hopeless future. After all, he was not just a valiant soldier protecting his homeland but also a mighty general in the service of the king! Surely something could be done for him. He was a leader, a mover and shaker of the ancient world! He was rich in gold and silver with many changes of fine clothes. He had sheep and cattle, land, slaves, the most beautiful wife in the land (second only to the queen, if the king should ask).

But disease is no respecter of men, and leprosy afflicted his body just as if he were a common man, creating open sores that oozed and would not heal. Pain ravaged his body with a constant ache and sharp pinching as his nervous system deteriorated in its fight against the incurable disease. He who had everything suddenly found himself with nothing to do but wait for death to take him.

He became desperate, willing to try anything. So finally:

Naaman went to his master and told him what the girl from Israel had said. "By all means, go," the king of Aram replied. "I will send a letter to the king of Israel." So Naaman left, taking with him ten talents of silver, six thousand shekels of gold and ten sets of clothing. The letter that he took to the king of Israel read: "With this letter I am sending my servant Naaman to you so that you may cure him of his leprosy." (2 Kings 5:4–6)

With each step of his camel, Naaman felt the pain of each sore on his body. What was he thinking, following the advice of some foreign servant girl? Had he lost his mind? He was Naaman, the mighty warrior of the king, who had captured and slain more people than his little maid would ever meet in her life!

But he had no choice, did he? He was dying and desperate. There were no other options. His hope had evaporated just as quickly as energy drained from his body each day. The sun blazed above him, and he adjusted the flaxen scarf loosely draped around his head and neck. He wasn't sure he would survive the journey to the cure. It seemed hopeless, but he kept going anyway. What else could he do?

Have you ever been so desperate that you were willing to try anything? Have there been times you wrestled

with your pride because you couldn't believe that anything—
or anyone—could help you?

The mighty war hero Naaman knew what this inner battle felt like. He became so desperate that when his wife told
him what her maid had said, he took notice. Someone in Israel—of all places—who could heal him? Really? With no
time to lose, he went straight to the king: if anyone could
connect him with this prophet, this man who healed in the
name of their God, then surely the king of Aram could. And
sure enough, the king sent word to Elisha and directed Naaman to the prophet's house.

He showed up at Elisha's house with all his chariots and
horses (in case someone couldn't tell that he was a very important man), and now finally, he was getting somewhere.
He'd found the man his wife's maid had told him about, the
one who might be able to heal him. But instead of this man
Elisha coming out to greet him and acknowledge how very
important he was, then heal him, the so-called healer sent a
messenger out to tell him to go dip in the Jordan seven times.

DESPITE THE OPEN SORES ON HIS BODY, NAAMAN HAD
*tried to dress like the important military leader he was. His only
addition was a loose scarf around his face to hide the ravages of this
hellish affliction. The angry, red welts had spread to his neck and*

were now visible on his cheeks and ears. Traveling so far from home had not helped him. He still couldn't believe that he had come all the way to Israel on the advice of some little slave girl. But his wife had insisted. She had become convinced that their maid knew something or, better yet, knew someone.

Now here he stood in front of this man Elisha's house. He was not impressed—the place looked rather small and in need of a bit of repair. He really was stooping beneath himself, compromising his dignity, in order to go chasing after the wind. What could a man who lived in a place like this possibly have to give him, one of the most powerful generals in all of history?

Finally, the strange Hebrew man, this so-called prophet who received messages from this almighty God of theirs, sent a servant out to deliver his message. Really—a servant? To greet him after the distance he had traveled? Why, the man wasn't even willing to come out and offer basic hospitality—water for the camels and re-freshment for him and his retinue. And then when Elisha's servant delivered his master's message, it was beyond comprehension!

Of all the nerve! *Naaman fumed.* Doesn't he know who I am? And telling me to bathe in the Jordan River, of all places! There are much finer waters in Damascus closer to home! *Enraged, he stormed away. If this was the way they treated people in need of help, he didn't need them!*

* * *

Do you get the impression that Naaman would fit right in on one of our present-day reality shows? He definitely had the ego for it! He must've been beside himself, thinking about Elisha's response to his predicament. While everyone at home would've fallen all over themselves to do anything, *anything*, he asked, Elisha gave him no preferential treatment. He could've been the king himself or a servant, but Elisha simply told Naaman what he must do if he wanted to be healed.

It appears he would have just gone home with his pride intact but his body falling apart. However, once again, servants intervened. And I can just hear them, in this case wiser than their master, telling him to calm down, take a breath, and count to ten. They even used a little psychology. They knew that often a little shift in perspective can make a big shift in attitude.

"Master," they said, "just think about this for a minute. If the healer had asked you to go to the pyramids in Egypt and obtain eucalyptus from a sealed tomb to rub on your body, surely you would have set off in pursuit of such a cure. But how fortunate! All you have to do is go to the Jordan nearby and wash seven times. This is good news!"

Once again, it's his servants, the people behind the scenes, the ones whose names are not even mentioned, who save him. "Naaman's servants went to him and said, 'My father, if the prophet had told you to do some great thing, would you not have done it? How much more, then, when he tells you, 'Wash and be cleansed'!" (2 Kings 5:11–13). I imagine they communicated a whole lot more: "I know you are a great man, but from all appearances, sir, you are too in need to be insulted. You cannot allow *who you are* to get in the way of *what you need*! This is the cure for your incurable disease! This is not hard, sir. It's really quite simple, and sometimes *the simple* is what releases *the supernatural*, and that is precisely what *you* have got to have.

"You need a miracle, my lord! We need a miracle! Whatever is eating away at you must stop now! We are in it with you. We are for you. You are not just any leader, you are *our* leader. You are not just any captain, you are *our* captain. You are a gifted, skilled, brave man. You have that mysterious edge about you that enables you to make a difference in the lives of people. And we need you, sir. Oh, how we need you! So, if you won't do it for *you*, will you please do it for *us*?"

Amazingly, they cared about more him than his title and wealth and importance. They wanted to show him the basic human kindness they would show anyone. They wanted him to know that *his life* made a huge impact on *their lives*. They wanted him to take off his title and pride long enough to slow down and get the help he needed.

Who helps keep you grounded and accountable and humble? Who reminds you of God's presence in your life when you start to slip into thinking too high or too low of yourself? Who provides you with a sense of God's healing when you need it?

If it weren't for the "little" people in Naaman's life, he would have died!

Miraculously, as Naaman rose from dipping in the Jordan the seventh time, his sores disappeared. His body had been cleansed of the leprosy consuming his flesh. We're told his skin was like that of a young boy! He also came out of the water a believer in this God of the Hebrews. His external condition had been healed and his internal disease of pride had also been washed away.

When our pride is washed from us, we are often healed from a number of our infirmities. Our pride can make our hearts hard and our souls sour. Sometimes, like Naaman, we must go to a place that's familiar and ordinary, a place we might even think is beneath us. God will do whatever it takes to humble us so that we turn our hearts to him instead of our wealth, position, or fame. Humility is in us even when we can't find it. Sometimes we just have to trust God to wash away everything that it's hiding behind.

THE REPETITION ANNOYED HIM AT FIRST. ONCE, TWICE . . . finally, seven times. What was the point? To humiliate him further? Hadn't he already embarrassed himself by coming to this strange

*place and begging to be healed? But his questions and embarrass-
ment and pride seemed to wash away with each dip into the mighty
Jordan. Something was happening . . . did he dare to think . . .
could it be?*

*Rising out of the water the seventh time, Naaman felt re-
born. The sun on his skin felt wonderful, and it took him a moment to realize that there was no pain. And then as his eyes
scanned his body—no, it wasn't possible! Tears sprung from his
eyes as waves of joy matched the waves of the Jordan now lapping
at his knees.*

*He stumbled to the riverbank and could not stop weeping. He
had not felt so strong, so healthy, since he was a young man of
twenty. Glory to the God of Israel! And praise be to this God for
sending Naaman his beautiful messenger—the wonderful young
woman in his household! She had saved him. Along with his other
servants, she and her holy man Elisha and their God of all power.
Praise him!*

THERE'S SO MUCH FOR US TO LEARN FROM THE STORY OF
Naaman's maid. First, if you want to make a difference in
the world, remain faithful in the midst of adversity. Whether
you're a college student, a young professional, a newlywed,
an empty nester, a divorced single parent, a retired senior, or
one of the many military families who make sacrifices daily to

protect those of us who live in the land of the free, we all face challenges in our lives.

Naaman had leprosy; what's "eating" you and leaving you isolated and hopeless? Are you allowing your pride to get in the way of God's solution that's right before you? Is your ego too big to fit through the door of opportunity that's just been opened? Naaman's kind of pride and entitlement can infect every area of your life.

At home we face relational tension with our spouse or rebellion from our kids. At work we must handle more responsibility with less support, along with angry bosses who don't play fair and coworkers who care only about their next promotion. At church we long to worship as part of a community and yet we always seem to come away longing for something just out of reach.

Or maybe your adversity is greater and more similar to that of the young woman enslaved in a culture the opposite of her own. Maybe you feel exiled from your family and friends for taking a stand about what's important to you and your faith. Perhaps you've lost your job and your savings are quickly evaporating. Maybe you're struggling with a secret addiction—shopping, hoarding, gambling, drinking, taking prescription painkillers, or surfing for porn. Maybe you're caring for someone you love who's dying of cancer. Maybe someone you hold near and dear to your heart has been stricken with Alzheimer's. Day by day, a part of that person you cherish packs up and moves far away, and you're living with the reality that you may never see that part of them again.

Whatever the adversity you face, you can still remain faithful to the God who loves you. He has not abandoned you, just as he never left this young woman who became Naaman's maid. He hurts when you hurt. He continues to provide for you, whether it's this month's mortgage payment or the emotional support you need to leave an abusive situation. God is always faithful.

A key to surviving this situation is working hard and remaining obedient to God on a consistent basis, no matter what feelings may come. Take the responsibilities you have as seriously as you can and do your earnest best to fulfill them. Refuse to act on any feelings of self-pity, and surprise others with your positive attitude and willingness to serve. Do what you know to do, no matter how small it may seem. Just take the next step and then the next one and the one after that.

When you live this way, you can trust God for the outcome in his timing. Maybe you won't get the job you just applied for, but it could lead you to the place where God wants you. Not having the financial resources you once did may force you to rely on God in ways that will put your faith on spiritual steroids! Without diminishing or trivializing the hardships you may be facing, you must look for God's hand leading you to a stronger place in your relationship with him.

Finally, we must remain humble if we are to unlock all that God has placed within us. The moment we think that we deserve special treatment—whether it's getting a table without a reservation or feeling superior to the homeless person we pass on the street—we have stepped into Naaman's shoes. We are all God's children and deserve the same love and respect that he shows to each of us. We are told not only to love our neighbors as ourselves but to love our enemies as well.

The scent of dried figs filled the kitchen as she looked out the window once again. It had been many days since her master had gone back to her homeland. How she missed her family in Israel, how she longed to worship in the temple again. But the Lord permitted her to be here, in Naaman's house, and she knew it was for a reason. She knew it was so the Lord could save his life.

As soon as she saw her master's traveling party coming toward the house, she saw his smile and knew that his trip had been successful. She knew in her heart that her prayers had been answered and her master had been healed. She ran to the door and could not wait to see for herself what God had done.

And then to see him standing there! Her master's skin was smooth and clear of the disease that had plagued him for so long. He even looked younger, like a boy almost, with his ruddy glow and the mysterious twinkle in his eyes. There was something different about him, not just that his skin was without blemish. Somehow she sensed that he had changed on the inside as well.

She dared not speak to him first as he entered the house. He went immediately to his wife, and they cried together over this miracle. As their tears of joy subsided, they whispered and then her master called her.

He hugged her then, as if she were his own daughter, and looked her in the eye. "Thank you," he whispered in her ear. "Thank you for giving me a gift that I didn't deserve."

"Thanks be to God," she whispered.

THE STORY OF BEING "MORE THAN A MAID" REMINDS US that no matter how hard your life feels, God can use you to bless others. No matter how young, small, insignificant you may feel, you can change people's lives through your faith. God loves to use the underdogs, the prostitutes like Rahab, the poor widow like Ruth, the young woman like Naaman's little maid, to advance his mighty kingdom.

She was a daughter of Abraham and remained true to herself and her God while tucked away in an idolatrous house. God used her to save Naaman's life. We hope that when Naaman got his miracle, he did not forget about her. Through her, God gave him victory, freedom, life . . . he should have compensated her to return to her homeland with gifts to dwell among her own people. She was a spoil of war who became a hero to be treasured. Her story is almost swallowed up in his big life, but the truth of the matter is you can't accurately tell his story without telling hers. This little lady was much more than a maid, she was the key to one of the greatest miracles in the Bible: not just the physical healing of a powerful man, but the internal healing of a wounded soul.

We don't have to work to be important. God values each one of us and has given us a special, unique role in the work of his kingdom. People may not appreciate us. They may overlook and ignore us. But we must remain faithful and testify to God's power and goodness by how we treat them in return. We don't have to impress or "one up" them with how we look or where we live or the car we drive. We simply have to remain as hopeful, as compassionate, and as bold as Naaman's little maid.

You may not think you have it in you—the patience needed to endure adversity, the power required to overcome your circumstances, the compassion necessary to love those who challenge or oppress you. And yet Naaman's maid shows us that anyone who is willing to remain faithful and humble can become a pivot point for grace, a turning point for healing, and a power point for God's ability to do miracles.

CHAPTER EIGHT

COAT OF CONFIDENCE

A BEAUTIFUL OLDER WOMAN OF GOD, A MEMBER OF MY church, was praying one day about what she should do with the quilt she had just completed. The Lord told her to take her incredible hand-sewn work of art and give it to her pastor—me! What an amazing gift to receive out of the blue!

When she asked to meet with me, I had no idea what she had in mind. Even when she presented me with the large bundle wrapped in black plastic and tied with a bow, I didn't realize the enormous treasure waiting inside. Opening the package, I couldn't believe my eyes. The beautiful quilt spilled out, red blocks framed by blue borders with rings of patchwork petals within each square.

I studied the intricate beauty of all the different fabrics brought together into this spectacular design. There were prints and stripes, cottons and silks, florals and flannel, all blooming together inside the gorgeous garden of fabric this precious woman had quilted. Each block of fabric seemed to tell a story from this woman's life.

And at a vibrant eighty-three years old, this lovely lady clearly had plenty of stories to tell. She still works, still drives, and even takes care of "an older friend," a woman who's well over a hundred! Through her gift, she welcomed me into years of her life and dozens of seasons of her life.

Like a beautiful mosaic, her quilt unites a myriad of wildly different pieces that on their own would be considered nothing more than rags. But brought together by the stitches of a master quilter, the diverse fabrics form an amazing piece of practical art.

Her gift reminds me that sometimes life seems like one big crazy quilt! Can you relate? One thing happens and then another, a surprising blessing followed by a painful loss. Individually, I might be tempted to isolate each piece and lose perspective on the whole. But God sews them together with a precision and a beauty that I could never manage on my own. He shows me that all the pieces come from inside me and that all are necessary, even the painful ones, in order to become his masterpiece.

No one knew what it was like to live a crazy-quilt life better than a young man named Joseph, a dreamer whose destiny demanded that he discover what God had placed inside of him. When we think of Joseph, we usually think about him as a hero. After all, he became the second most powerful leader in Egypt and saved his family, along with that entire region of the world, from starvation when a severe drought hit.

Yet he also went through long periods of preparation, waiting, and suffering before any of his major accomplishments could come to fruition. He experienced lows that would seem to scrape the bottom of his patience and resilience, only to be followed by something worse. He had to accumulate a lot of painful fabrics before God combined them to produce an intricate masterpiece.

HE COULDN'T UNDERSTAND WHY HIS BROTHERS TREATED him so poorly. Sure, he was younger than all but one of them—a mere "baby," as they liked to tease—but their contempt for him ran deeper. Maybe their father did show him a bit more favor than the others, but surely they knew how much their father loved each of them. Then there was the coat—that bright, beautiful, silly coat with its stripes and swatches of woven cloth in every color of the rainbow. Stripes as blue as the morning sky. Patches of green like ripe olives. Streaks of red like the juice of the pomegranate. Bursts of yellow and orange like the sun. Purple thread binding all the pieces together.

The coat made him feel special, and he loved wearing it. His brothers didn't care what they wore, but Joseph's father knew that his youngest son would cherish a garment as unique as this one. Joseph wore it everywhere he went and found that it kept him cool in the blazing scorch of the afternoon sun or warm on a chilly, starless night.

And to tell the truth, Joseph knew he was special. He knew he was destined for great things. He knew he would travel and meet kings and conquerors, see the foreign lands beyond the sea. For as long as he could remember, he knew that God had blessed him and placed within him something rare and precious. And he had dreams—oh, the dreams—that would reveal pictures of his destiny.

The latest one had been especially vivid. He was standing on a hill that towered above the land and elevated him into the clouds. There, as he surveyed his surroundings, he saw the sun and the moon and the stars gathered at his feet, as if bowing before him. It was a strange dream—perhaps even stranger than the previous one, in which he and his brothers were binding sheaves of wheat out in a field. His sheaf of wheat had risen out of his hands while his brothers' sheaves fell down before it.

Of course, his family didn't like hearing about his dreams. And maybe he was naïve to think that his brothers would appreciate them. They were already jealous, so the last thing they wanted to hear was that their baby brother would be elevated above them in some way. But even Joseph's father, Jacob, chided him for sharing this latest dream. "Who do you think you are, my son, that we, your family, would ever bow down before you? You are no king! Now get back to work." His father scowled at him, ruffling his hair in a playful way that made Joseph smile even as he returned to the fields with his brothers. (Genesis 37, 39–45)

AS WE SEE IN JOSEPH'S STORY, WHEN THE MARK OF GOD IS on your life, there can be definite dreams, or visions, associated with it. But be careful with whom you share them, because along with every God-given concept comes an "assassin" who wants to smother it before you can ever bring it to life.

What idea is in you that seems to threaten or intimidate those around you? How do you keep your vision alive when those around you plot to destroy you for it? How do you protect your heart in the middle of others who want to put you down? Joseph's siblings were sick and tired of their kid brother's dreams of greatness. So one day, when they saw him coming, they plotted to kill him—thereby killing his grandiose expectations as well. I'm guessing you know exactly what it's like to have others gunning for you, eager to shoot you down for even daring to see a bright future for yourself.

Whether you have office coworkers spreading gossip to prevent your promotion or family members who refuse to celebrate the gifts God has so obviously given you, we've all experienced people who try to snuff out the spark of destiny in our hearts. We must realize that as we discover what God has placed inside of us, others may not celebrate our discovery. But this is no reason to give up! When God places his seeds of greatness in your heart, you must protect them and help them grow—even in adverse conditions.

As we see with Joseph, there's a real flip side to having a sense of destiny and discovering what God has placed within you. On the one side, there's blessing, but on the other side, there are persecution and suffering. Joseph was moved out from under his father's watchful eye and into the hands of his begrudging brothers. He found himself at the mercy of resentful family members who had no idea that the favor on their brother's life was the same favor that would one day keep them alive in a time of severe need.

Have you ever had to endure the threats and persecution of others in order to keep your expected destiny alive? It may have been family members who were jealous, coworkers who didn't understand, or friends who resented your success. All of us will face adversity from other people, but we must never allow their barriers to stop our forward progress. When God is for us, it doesn't matter who is against us!

THEY HAD TAKEN IT TOO FAR THIS TIME. NOT ONLY HAD they taken his coat of many colors, but they had dropped him into this pit, this dry well. He was hungry and thirsty and tired and he wanted to go home. Just wait until their father heard what his brothers had done to him. They would be sorry. He could still hear their voices in the distance. They had tried to scare him with all their talk of killing him. He understood that they were jealous and that he should quit telling them his dreams. But this stunt of theirs was totally uncalled for.

When they lowered a rope for him, he thought that finally, their joke had come to end. He wouldn't show them how upset he was or let them know about the tears that had silently poured down his face in the pit of darkness. He would play along and try to be a good sport until they got home. But then he would run to Jacob and tell him what they had done, and boy, would they be sorry.

But, as he discovered at the top of the well, he wouldn't be going home. As his eyes adjusted to the bright, blinding sun, he looked up and saw strangers, Ishmaelite traders on their camels, talking with his brothers. They handed his brother Judah some pieces of silver and then they came for him. Reuben was not there—surely he had gone for their father—and the others did not speak to him. They wouldn't even look at him. They bound him like a lamb to be slaughtered at the time of sacrifices.

"My brothers—what, what are you doing? You've taken the joke too far," Joseph said and then realized what was happening. "No—no!" A calloused hand stuffed a burlap rag into his mouth to smother his cries. He was led to the band of traders and secured behind one of them on the back of a camel. The tears came again and he could do nothing but let them fall.

Have you found yourself in the "pit" of life? How did you respond? We sometimes, like Joseph, go from the frying pan into the fire! He went from being at the bottom of the pit to being sold into slavery!

When we climb out of one pit, we often think that we shouldn't have to face any more problems for a while. We think, *Oh, thank you, Lord! I'm so glad you rescued me. And I'm so looking forward to a nice long vacation at the beach!* We want life to go smoothly and easily for us, and honestly, it rarely does. Pain, persistence, and patience seem to be the recipe for maturity.

Or perhaps you often find yourself attempting a strategy that Joseph's brothers used. Without him strutting around in his bright coat describing his latest prophetic dream, Joseph and all his special favor would be a thing of the past, a distant memory. This strategy—out of sight, out of mind—tends to be the way many envious people deal with those who are marked by destiny. The sad thing is that often they are so busy trying to interfere with someone else's divine appointment that they miss their own.

But Joseph's favor went with him into slavery in the land of Egypt. Despite all of his brothers' best efforts to keep him down, he was raised to a position of power. The Bible reveals that, even in his enslaved condition, "he was a prosperous man" (Gen. 39:2). His new master, Potiphar, couldn't help but notice that everything Joseph touched became blessed. Therefore, like any good leader, Potiphar gave Joseph more responsibility and made him overseer of his house, placing him in charge of everything in the captain's home.

It's important for us to realize that even in adverse circumstances, Joseph still experienced the Lord's favor. Why? Because he remained faithful and didn't become a victim, feeling sorry for himself and giving up hope of God's redemption. He knew that God had not abandoned him even in his unexpected tribulations. Our Father never forsakes us, even when our world seems to crash around us and those we hold dearest shock us with their ability to hate and their attempts to destroy us.

Clearly Joseph's attitude was not that of a victim who suffered his captivity with bitterness, anger, laziness, and disrespect. Instead Joseph made the most of the situation, even though he would never have chosen his challenging circumstances. Like Naaman's little maid, who was taken as a prisoner of war and made to be a slave, Joseph could see beyond his confinement, beyond the pain of his brothers' devastating betrayal.

When the favor of God has marked your life, it doesn't matter where anyone places you because you will always rise to the top. Furthermore, even though you might be in a difficult situation, God may bless everyone and everything around you because *of you.* "The Lord blessed the Egyptian's house for Joseph's sake; and the blessing of the Lord was upon all that he had in the house, and in the field" (Gen. 39:5).

Even as you're moving forward into your divine destiny, it sometimes feels as if you're going backward. But even when he was wrongly accused of a crime, Joseph never gave up.

Forced to serve an unjust sentence, he again rose to the top. He found favor with those in charge of the prison and was given responsibilities and rights that positioned him above the other inmates. Again, even in prison of all places, Joseph experienced the favor of the Lord upon him so that the warden didn't feel the need to check up on this foreigner (Gen. 39:21–23).

HE COULD NO LONGER REMEMBER HOW MANY YEARS HAD passed since he was sold by his brothers and brought into Egypt by the traders. The traders had not mistreated him and in fact were almost kind to him. Joseph knew that despite what his brothers had done to him, God was still with him. Their terrible betrayal had not stolen his gift, the one from the Lord himself, the destiny that was his future.

And God continued to show him favor in the midst of adversity. The traders sold him to Pharaoh's captain of the guard, a tall Egyptian named Potiphar. His new master also treated him very well and showed an appreciation for Joseph's hard work, eye for detail, and conscientious efforts. Joseph always gave more than others expected of him.

When his efforts prospered with those tasks, soon Joseph found himself in charge of Potiphar's entire household. He supervised other servants, kept the schedule of events and special meals, recommended the menus, and purchased the household items needed— wheat, grapes, figs, goat's milk, wine, oil, and barley.

The only challenge was his master's wife. She buzzed around him like a perfumed bee, constantly flirting and smiling and teasing. At first, he thought she was just being kind to him, but then one day in the storeroom, she had leaned in close and whispered something that made his face blush with shame. He had said nothing in reply and immediately left her presence. And since that day, the woman had made many similar remarks. She was a beautiful woman who dressed in silks and finery, as befitting the wife of Pharaoh's captain. But her lustful eyes and seductive smile made her ugly, made her look like a ravenous she-lion always on the prowl for more prey.

Joseph managed to steer clear of Mrs. Potiphar until she set the trap that would send him to prison. He blushed even to remember her coarse words and unholy invitation. Despite his successful efforts to escape her intentions, her lying accusations stuck to him like honey. Potiphar was outraged and had Joseph thrown into Pharaoh's prison. And as he was led away, his accuser looked at him with a vengeful smile that made him furious on the inside.

Sitting in his jail cell, he could only wonder why the Lord had allowed such a thing to happen. Wasn't he already doing his best in a terrible situation—betrayed by his brothers, exiled from his homeland, enslaved by foreigners? Now to be falsely accused and imprisoned. No, he would not lose hope. God would show him the way. No matter what happened, no matter what other people did, he would not let them take his faith. His confidence was in the Lord and the Lord alone.

Joseph thought of the beautiful coat his father had once given him and smiled. He no longer had the coat, but the confidence it had given him remained. The colors God had placed within him would never fade.

HAVE YOU EVER WONDERED WHEN YOUR TRIALS WOULD finally be over and you could get on with your life? Maybe you've struggled with a life-threatening disease or injury, and just as you improved and looked forward to a full recovery, some setback sent you reeling. Or maybe it's healing from a friend's betrayal. Just as things begin to improve with one friend, a different one betrays you in even worse ways. Or maybe you quit your job to take a better position with another company, only to be laid off a year later when the economy slumped.

By the time he was thirty, Joseph was still serving time for a crime he didn't commit. Thirteen years had passed since he'd been thrown into the pit by his brothers. Yet these were years of faithfulness on Joseph's part, in spite of what he had gone through. And now favor was about to promote him yet again: Pharaoh himself commanded that the Hebrew prisoner be brought before him.

You see, Joseph had interpreted the dream of a fellow prisoner, the Pharaoh's butler, and asked the butler to remember him when he returned to his master's good graces. But the butler forgot and Jacob sat in jail another couple of years. I'm convinced that God allowed the butler to forget about Joseph until the divine timing was right for the fulfillment of his destiny. God was about to restore to Joseph all that the enemy had stolen, all that jealousy, malice, and revenge had consumed.

You never know when God will surprise you by bringing fruit from a seed you've planted, even one you planted a long time ago and may have forgotten about. As God tells us in his

Word: "And I will restore to you the years that the locust hath eaten, the cankerworm, and the caterpillar, and the palmerworm, my great army which I sent among you. And you shall eat in plenty, and be satisfied" (Joel 2:25–26).

Did Joseph recognize the window of opportunity that God was opening before him? I wonder if he knew, standing before Pharaoh, that he was about to enter his God-given destiny. The Bible says that after leaving the prison and before standing in front of Pharaoh, Joseph changed his clothes. He knew that he could not go into his future wearing the old garments of the past. But did he ever dream that soon he would be wearing the finest clothes in his new royal role? Could he have imagined the leap he was about to make into all that God had for him?

And what about you? Are you ready to take the next step in fulfilling your destiny? If an opportunity knocked at your door today, would you be ready to respond?

Joseph was! And I believe it's because he had never lost hope. He never lost his faith, even as he faced one thing after another. His trust in God brought him to his appointment with destiny. Opportunity knocks when we least expect it, but if we continue to seek God, regardless of our circumstances, we will be ready when the time presents itself. Joseph was prepared for *anything* because he had been faithful through *everything*!

Up until this moment, Joseph's favor had taken him from a pit to slavery, and from slavery to imprisonment. His freedom had been a long time coming, but the Bible says, "A man's gift makes room for him, and brings him before great men" (Prov. 18:16). This is exactly what Joseph experienced. His gift of interpretation and his commitment to God's faithfulness led him from the pits of the prison to the peaks of the palace.

The favor that had accompanied him throughout his life was about to propel him into the fullness of his true identity and his divine destiny. Pharaoh told Joseph his dream, and God revealed the interpretation through Joseph. As a result, Pharaoh appointed Joseph not only in charge of the harvests, but also as ruler over all the land, second only to the esteemed leader himself! Pharaoh even gave Joseph a ring to signify his status as ruling leader (Gen. 41:14–44).

With the mark of purpose on his life and the ring of authority on his finger, Joseph stepped into his appointment with destiny so that he could preserve a multitude of people. Pharaoh's dream became a reality just as Joseph had foretold.

When your moment before Pharaoh occurs, you want to be ready. And in order to be ready, you must never lose faith and distance yourself from God. No matter how hard your life may become, never allow yourself to give up on God's ability to transform it into something beyond your imagination. He knows what's inside you even when you think you've hit rock bottom.

For a moment, he said nothing, for he was truly without words. Standing in front of him were his own brothers— older, thinner, haggard, gaunt even. They looked weary and defeated, clearly humbled by the famine and having to come hundreds of miles in order to beg for bread—not once, but twice now. He had enjoyed playing his little games with them and felt no guilt for wanting to test them and their motives.

And they still didn't recognize him at all. But now the time was at hand. He tore the Egyptian headdress away and stripped off his outer royal tunic. He ran his hands through his hair and cried out like a wounded animal, "Can you really see me and not know who I am? I am Joseph—your brother! The one you tried to destroy, to abandon, to enslave, to imprison with your hatred!" His tears flowed like a waterfall then and his pain coursed through him like a river through the desert.

Do you know that you're a survivor? And not only a survivor, but a thriver as well! You may not feel as though you have the tenacity to endure your current circumstances, but you do. God's placed it there, just as he placed it inside of Joseph. You may not feel you have the faith to remain resilient in the face of adversity, but you do.

If anyone knew firsthand what it takes to be a survivor, surely it was Joseph. Survival became the very essence of his spirit. Yet little did he know that through his own spirit of survival, he would save his own family as well as millions of others.

Hit after hit, blow after blow, what had kept Joseph motivated to press onward? Only the call of God and the favor so evident in his life could sustain him beyond the deadly detours that were intended to derail his destiny. When others mishandled him, Joseph remained steadfast in the hands of the Lord. Because God had a strong hold on his life, in the end, what was meant to shove him around ultimately pushed him into his purpose.

The same is true for us. I'm convinced that this is often how God works in our lives. What our enemies intend as a push becomes God's pull toward our destiny. Your boss may think he's firing you, but really he's lighting a fire within that will send you to an even better job. Your friend may think she's putting you in your place, but she's only putting you in position so you can receive the loyalty of a better friend. Others may think they're robbing us, but we know they are only making room for the bounty of blessings that God has waiting for us.

In the midst of our largest losses and most devastating detours, we must realize that God is all-powerful and all-knowing—all the time. We may not be able to imagine coming out of the shadows of our grief, but he knows how to lead us back into the light. We may not fathom how we could ever laugh again, but already our Father is smiling at us. We may not be able to dream of ever loving again after losing someone, but God knows there's a wellspring of hope within us that can never run dry.

JOSEPH COULD NOT BELIEVE THAT HIS BROTHERS WERE really standing before him. He had tested them and they had passed. They, too, had changed over the years. God had been working their lives just as he had in Joseph's. He could stand it no more; it was time for the healing between them to begin. He had finally spoken the words he had dreamed of saying for so many years.

His brothers stood as still as stones. They were afraid. Never in their wildest dreams did they imagine meeting him again. No, he was always the dreamer. And his dream from so long ago had come true. But he could not hate them. Oddly, he felt only compassion for them. They had tried so hard to bring about his destruction, which, amazingly enough, God had used as the building blocks of his greatness.

He drew his brothers close to him and embraced them. Then he forgave them. God still knew how to surprise him—this time with the greatest gift of his life.

JOSEPH WAS BORN KNOWING HE WAS SPECIAL, BUT HE never knew all he had in him until circumstances tried to crush him. He didn't know that his confidence in the Lord would sustain and elevate him to a position where he would save millions of lives.

He didn't know that his sensitivity to the Lord would allow him to interpret dreams and that this would serve as his key to freedom. He didn't know he had the capacity to forgive those people—his own brothers—who had hurt him so deeply. But God knew it was there, just waiting to come out.

God knows what's inside you as well. The trial or painful circumstance that ensnares you right now may feel like a prison sentence. But we must never lose hope that he is orchestrating even the bad things into catalysts for his kingdom. Even when our world becomes black and white, as long as we have our coat of confidence, we will experience God's favor in living color.

CHAPTER NINE

WHAT A DIFFERENCE A DAY MAKES

W HEN YOU WERE A CHILD, DID YOU EVER IMAGINE that you would be where you are now in life? More important, do you realize you're still in the process of fulfilling your divine potential? Too often we reach a point in life where we begin to feel as if our heartfelt, full-throttle, this-is-what-I'm-made-for life is over. We may think back on our "glory days" when we were in high school and won the beauty pageant or the big state tournament title.

You may remember when you met your spouse and how

incredible it was to fall in love, then celebrate the wedding of your dreams. Maybe you recall when you first started your job and still felt as though you could conquer the world with your new ideas and unquenchable passion for success. Or when your kids were small, and things seemed so simple; sure, there may not have been much money, but looking back, you now see those days as the happiest of your life.

We start out in life full of hope and promise, and then, well, life happens to us. We start to realize that those early experiences didn't guarantee that our lives would be one long string of successes. We discover that marriage takes hard work, and office politics often poison even the most dynamic workplaces. We experience the challenges of child rearing and become battered and sometimes embittered by life's blows, bullies, and bills.

When we're struggling, it's tempting to look back with rose-tinted glasses and begin to wonder if the best has already been and the rest is just a matter of coasting down from that mountaintop. And this season of sliding, this nostalgic notion of nothing-new-can-happen-now, tends to leave us a little jaded or even cynical. It may leave us numb behind the veneer of a practiced smile or a well-rehearsed "I'm blessed—how are you?"

As our lives unfold, we often begin to question our

anointing or doubt our destiny. Our patience begins to wear thin as our early hopes and dreams begin to seem like childish notions. We wonder if God has forgotten about us, and we question whether we really understood his promise to us when we were younger. Surely if we were becoming the man or woman of God that he created us to be, there would be more abundance in our lives and more passion in our souls, right?

At various junctures in my life when I've asked myself this same question, I've remembered how much I loved fairy tales when I was a little girl. They not only stirred my imagination with stories of princesses and wicked queens, dwarfs and fairy godmothers, but they also helped me appreciate that things are not what they appear to be. A little old grandmother may turn out to be the big bad wolf, or a young woman in filthy rags may become the belle of the ball. And I loved happy endings, knowing that underdogs could save the day and the prince could find the rightful owner of a dropped glass slipper.

As I grew older, I discovered that I loved the true stories in the Bible even more. Some of the same amazing kinds of situations appear in the Bible—only they actually happened! And as an adult, I've been sustained and nourished over and over by the very stories we've been exploring together in this book. Whether it's the grace to start over that I witness in

Ruth or the faithful obedience of Noah and his wife, I'm inspired to remember that God is *always* up to something in our lives.

Our lives may appear to be mundane and uneventful on the surface, but God is still working out his purposes for the good of those who love him. And in the twinkling of an eye, he can reveal the truth of who we are and uncover the power he's placed within us. And if he reveals our true identity to us early in life, we must never forget that anointing, even if it seems it couldn't be further from where we find ourselves now.

One of my favorite people in the Bible, who clearly knew something about this process of knowing and waiting, is David. From being the forgotten baby brother to the anointed one chosen by God to be Israel's next king, from being the naïve shepherd boy to becoming the fearless giant-slayer, David knew what a difference a day can make.

His humble beginnings and selection by God remind us that we, too, don't know what's on the next page of our lives. We may think that our most exciting moments have passed, but David reminds us that God's best is often yet to come. His anointing on our lives is real, and he is faithful to keep his promises. It may not feel as though we're moving into our divine destiny, but God knows where's he leading us, just as surely as David knew where to lead the sheep he tended.

The prophet awakened and heard God speaking to him: "Samuel, it is time to turn a page in the history of my chosen nation, Israel. I'm through with King Saul and his disobedience. I have rejected him. Get your anointing oil and journey to Bethlehem. Find a man by the name of Jesse. I have chosen one of his sons to become the next king."

In obedience to the Lord, the prophet gathered the oil and a few provisions and set out for the countryside. Bethlehem was just a backwoods little town, full of farmers and sheepherders, a few merchants, an inn or two. Was it really where God's next chosen king would be found? Samuel had learned not to question the Lord but to simply trust and obey the instructions he was given. If Yahweh said that the man he'd selected for the next leader of the nation was there in Bethlehem, that's where he must be!

On his journey, Samuel grew tired and hungry and had to stop and ask directions twice, but finally he arrived at Jesse's front door with the sacred oil in hand. As soon as he knocked, an older man with a long, gray-streaked, bushy beard came to the door and raised his eyebrows quizzically upon seeing the stranger.

"Are you Jesse? Excuse me, sir. I don't mean to intrude. It's just

that God has sent me here in search of Israel's next ruler. He told
me that he had marked one of your sons for kingship," Samuel said
confidently.

"Come in, sir," said Jesse. "Please, let me know how I can serve
our God in this matter. Would you like some water? I'll get you a
cool drink while I gather my sons together."

For a few seconds, Jesse could not begin to believe that this man
was actually serious. But something about his tone, his eyes, his
steady countenance, told Jesse that Samuel was indeed the prophet
of God sent to search for their country's next king.

Which seemed strange, really, since King Saul already had a son,
Jonathan, who everyone presumed would be the next king of Israel.
But who was Jesse to argue with God? So, like any excited father of
the God-appointed future king, he immediately called in his sons.
The young men lined up like prized cattle as Jesse handed Samuel a
clay cup filled with cool water from the cistern in the shade.

Samuel took one look at the tall and handsome Eliab and
thought, Ah, this must be the one! Surely he is the Lord's
choice. He looks the part, all right. He has that royal air
about him, that kingly quality of charisma.

But immediately Samuel felt the Lord reprove him and say,
"While men judge people's outward appearance, God looks at their
hearts. The appearance does not reveal what is lying deep in the
soul of a person."

Samuel closed his eyes in prayer for a moment and then re-
turned to studying the young men. Seven of Jesse's sons paraded

past Samuel, but one by one, the Lord refused them all. No matter how smart or handsome, how big and strong, how courageous or compassionate, none of them apparently had the quality that God needed for his next king.

The prophet scratched his head and wondered if he'd heard God's voice correctly. Lord, you did say Jesse's house in Bethlehem, didn't you? I'm in the right place, aren't I?

But God assured Samuel that this was indeed the right place. The prophet then turned and asked his host, "Do you have any other sons?"

Jesse started to shake his head and then his eyes lit up. "Well, there's my youngest—David. He's out in the field, taking care of my sheep. I'm not sure he's what you're looking for. Would you like to stay for dinner? We're having lamb chops!"

"Go get him—now! God has said that there's a king among your sons, and I can't stop searching until I find him. No, thank you—I don't want to stay for dinner! This is an urgent matter and we need to find this youngest boy of yours. I'm here on assignment and no one should be eating anything until our next king is found!" *(1 Samuel 16:1–13)*

ARE YOU ASSUMING THAT GOD CAN'T OR WON'T USE you in your present location? Maybe you live in a rural area, worship in a small church, and think God moves in major ways only in big, urban megachurches. You might be part of a large city church and think God works actively only in small towns or overseas in missions. David's story reminds us that no place is too small and no surprise too big for God's purposes.

Similarly, the people God chooses aren't the usual suspects. Have you resigned yourself to believing that God works only in the lives of the beautiful and wealthy and specially talented, those who appear godliest, the ones who look as if they have it together? Well, I'm here to burst your bubble, because we all need reminding that God looks far beyond what the human eye can see. He seems to delight in surprising us and using the underdogs—people like Gideon or Naaman's maid or David—to accomplish his purposes.

In fact, one of the consistent themes we see in the lives of those God chooses for greatness is to expect the unexpected. God loves turning our human perspective upside down and reminding us that we don't know everything—and maybe that we don't know anything! He knows that we're prone to get a little too big for our britches sometimes—or we get too fearful—and assume we know what he's thinking, where we're going, and how we'll get there. But that is not the case: there is always more to reality than meets the eye.

Like the other prophets God selected, Samuel had learned, perhaps the hard way, not to question God's instructions. He simply did what the Lord said and trusted God knew what he was doing. Certainly, heading to Bethlehem to anoint the next king may have caught Samuel by surprise. The current king appeared to have what was needed to lead God's people—he was authoritative, strong willed, and powerful. But apparently, something had changed within the man, and now God knew it was time for a change.

Is it time for you to change your expectations of God's presence in your life? We tend to form an image of what our lives will look like if we're walking with the Lord and stepping into our destiny. As a result, we end up making our attitude and our heart's participation conditional on the way things appear to be. We think, *If God is really leading us to his best, then my business should be more successful. If God is truly taking me to my divine destiny, then life shouldn't be so hard.*

But God never promised that our lives would be easy. In fact, I'm convinced that so much of how he prepares us for our greatness is through adversity. We hate to admit it, especially when we're in the middle of tough times, but trials force us to rely on God and strip away all the false idols and temporary crutches we have allowed ourselves to lean upon so heavily. When times are hard, we come back to the rock of our salvation and our all-powerful, sovereign King of kings.

Just because our ministry is small doesn't mean it won't change the world. Just because you don't look like a traditional business leader, don't doubt for a moment that God will prosper you. Just because you may not sound like all the other singers in the choir doesn't mean you shouldn't do a solo! God absolutely loves blowing our minds (and other people's) by surprising us with what he can do. If I had relied on other people's expectations of what a pastor looks like, then I would never have taken the steps of obedience to be where God wants me today. You only have to be yourself to become who you were meant to be!

JESSE WATCHED THE OLD PROPHET CAREFULLY AND WONdered what he must be thinking. What was he looking for, exactly? If he had to choose, which one of his sons would he choose to be the next king? Jesse thought, Now, let's see. Which of my boys has that specialness about him that would qualify him to be king? If I were God, it would have to be that one—after all, he's the best-looking. Not him? Well, then, it must be this one over here—he's the smartest one.

And then eventually there's none left. Their visitor asks if he has any more sons. "Well, there's no one . . . except little David."

But surely that's not who God wants as his next king! Why, he's only a boy! *David was his baby boy, everyone's kid brother, his teenaged wild woodsman out wrestling bears and mountain lions to protect the flock. Could he really be the one? No, surely not—he's still wet behind the ears!*

His sons looked at Jesse expectantly, still uncertain what their visitor was looking for. When he asked them to fetch David from the fields, they stood for a moment and looked even more puzzled. No one had ever considered the possibility that their youngest brother could be God's chosen king over all of Israel.

HAVE YOU EVER ENCOUNTERED A PERSON WHO BECAME A road-blocker on your life's journey? These people are often the critics who attack you with their cruel comments or gossipy chatter. They squash your dream by communicating, either directly or subtly, that you don't have what it takes. Maybe they're frustrated and hurting themselves or maybe they're just intimidated by your potential, but regardless of their motive they end up stalling your progress in the pursuit of your dream.

Road-blockers cause you to second-guess yourself. They may take the form of a teacher who gave you an F on your story because of poor grammar and said nothing about your wonderful creative abilities. Maybe it's the unintentional comment by a parent or loved one that suggested you'd never amount to much. It could be a coach, a pastor, or a boss who put you down at every opportunity or stole the credit that rightfully should have been yours.

We've all encountered these kinds of people; they slow us down or stop us for a while. And it may not even be intentional on their part. It's hard to believe that David's father could have been so inconsiderate of him. If it had been left up to Jesse, David would never have had his chance before God's ambassador. But the reality is that when God marks you, men will have to make room for you. People may have labeled you and can no longer see beyond the role you currently play. They may view you as "the boss" or "the salesman," "the mommy" or "the hostess," "the pretty one" or "the kid." And it may be hard for them to imagine you living beyond the label they have attached to you.

It's like when your kids are small and you're in the grocery store and happen to run into their third-grade teacher. All of a sudden it's a revelation that this person they know only as their teacher could be someone else's mommy! Their teacher could be a normal person who shops for breakfast cereal and orange juice just like everyone else!

But when God has chosen you for his purposes, it really doesn't matter how others see you or how they try to slow you down. David's father may not have intended to overlook his son. I doubt he was trying to be like Cinderella's wicked stepmother, who wanted to prevent the prince from finding her stepdaughter. But Jesse didn't see what God saw inside his youngest son. Where Jesse saw only the good-natured boy who loved the outdoors, God saw the makings of a king. God saw David's heart and knew how much he loved the Lord.

DAVID LOVED BEING OUTSIDE IN THE LUSH, GREEN MEAD-ows with the sheep at this time of the afternoon. It was where he felt closest to God. In fact, sometimes he himself felt like a sheep and that the Lord was his shepherd. And God was so good to him, leading him to the stream with the still waters, to rest and think and pray, to drink in all the joy and peace that he found there.

There was a rustle in the olive trees and sycamore behind him. He grabbed his slingshot and quickly turned. Surely a wild beast would not try to attack the flock in broad daylight!

Footsteps thundered down the hill toward him—his brothers. He counted three of them and wondered what had happened. Surely there was some calamity back home for them to run with such speed.

"Hey, David! Dad wants to see you back at the house—right now!" said his big brother Eliab.

Uh-oh. David asked, "Can't it wait? I'll be there in just a few hours, right after sundown."

"No, you can't wait until after sundown! Right now—come on!"

"Oh, great," David muttered. "What have I done now?" He

thought a minute and then called out, "What about the sheep? Who's going to watch them if I return to the house?"

"We'll watch the flock! Now stop with the questions already and go!"

David ran across the field and approached the door out of breath and smelling like sheep. Ruddy from the sun and wind, muddy from the rain and soil, he felt a bit self-conscious as he burst in and discovered his father and the rest of his brothers talking with a stranger. There was no time to wash his face and hands, no time to clean up and change his robe. Oh, well, if his father had called him in to meet this man, then it must be urgent.

Something tingled at the base of David's spine as he shook the hand of the man introduced as Samuel. It was as if lightning had seared him for a moment, and he had a sense that what was about to happen would change him for the rest of his life.

LITTLE DID DAVID KNOW THAT WHILE HE HAD BEEN faithfully tending his father's sheep, God had stripped the kingship from Saul and was now preparing to pass it to the young shepherd boy who had brought him so much pleasure. David had been appointed king before he knew anything about it. I wonder what God has done for you that you don't know anything about yet. What has he prepared for you that your eyes haven't yet seen and your ears haven't yet heard (1 Cor. 2:9)?

Whom has he spoken to on your behalf? Just because you haven't possessed it yet doesn't mean that he has not planned it.

Do you tend to make excuses when someone asks you to step forward? Are you afraid that you don't have the right education, the right wardrobe, the right social training to be a world changer?

I'm convinced that many people fail to walk through the doors that God opens for them because they're afraid they don't have what's required. They think that if they don't have a college degree they could never get the job. They believe that without an MBA they can't possibly become an entrepreneur and create a new product or service. They believe that without the right connections they'll never be able to land the new client. They think that because they don't have the right clothes or a certain look they can't rise to the top.

But if anyone reminds us that it's not about what's on the outside, it has to be David. There he was, about to experience the most pivotal moment of his entire life, and he wasn't dressed in a suit, hadn't had a haircut, and didn't smell very nice. David had no time to prepare himself for what was about to take place in his life. Purpose was pushing him from where he was to where he was destined to be.

Ready or not, the hour of his divine appointment with destiny had arrived.

Your divine hour of appointment is at hand as well! God doesn't care how many degrees you have, how much money is (or isn't) in the bank, how much credit card debt you're in, or what kind of car you drive. He doesn't care about when you had your last manicure or if you have the latest hairstyle. He doesn't look at the brand of your purse or the title below your name. He only looks at your heart. He only looks at all he has placed within you, at the treasure that is too often obscured by the trappings of success.

It's time to let go of all the false expectations and unnecessary conditions you've placed on yourself. It's time to let go of all the baggage of past mistakes and missed opportunities. It's time to move beyond the pitfalls of the past and the perfectionism of the present. It's time to keep your divine appointment with your God-given destiny!

As soon as Samuel saw David, he knew that he was indeed the choice of God. The boy didn't look as regal or as polished and poised as his older brothers. He was dirty and unkempt and smelled like the sheep he tended. But he was rosy-cheeked and tanned and comfortable with himself. He had a quick smile and a fiery light in his eyes. His greeting was warm and accepting, strong of body and gentle of spirit all at the same time. Yes, he was clearly the one.

Immediately after the young shepherd entered, God confirmed it beyond a doubt: "Get up and anoint him, for he is my chosen one, a man after my own heart." The young shepherd's brothers and father watched silently, curiously, hardly believing what was happening before their eyes.

While David was surrounded by his family, Samuel lifted the horn of oil and anointed the young man as God's next king of Israel. The room smelled of rosemary and hyssop and the other herbs crushed for the sacred oil. The young shepherd's eyes were closed and oil dripped from his forehead. When David opened his eyes finally, he smiled, and Samuel knew he was with a man who was favored by God like no one else he had ever met.

WHEN DAVID WOKE UP THAT MORNING, HE HAD NO IDEA how different his life would be by the end of the day. What a difference a day makes! One morning he's the youngest son of Jesse, a rough-and-tumble shepherd boy wrestling with his seven brothers. The next morning, he's still the same young man, and so much more. He's a king, a leader handpicked by God himself.

One of the things I love about David is that he doesn't seem to resist his anointing or make excuses. In sharp contrast to someone like Gideon with all his fleeces, David seemed to have no trouble whatsoever embracing the role God assigned him. There's no indication that he questioned Samuel or wondered if there'd been some mistake—even if perhaps his father and brothers did.

We don't witness any false modesty or an are-you-kidding-me attitude. Only a quiet celebration within his heart, I suspect. An acceptance of this huge step toward the fulfillment of all he had been created to be. A graceful response to a gracious invitation.

Do you respond to God's call more like Gideon or David? Do you struggle to grasp why God would choose you and keep asking for confirmation? Or do you display a calm confidence that enables you to don the garment of greatness that God is asking you to wear? My prayer for you is that David would be your model.

When you know that God is calling you to the next level, don't try his patience by dragging your feet and second-guessing his selection. He's God, after all—the lord of your life! As he picks you for his purposes, I hope you know, deep in your heart, that you are well on your way to being your best.

DAVID COULD STILL SMELL THE HERBS OF THE SACRED OIL, *even though it had been days since the prophet had anointed him as the chosen one, the man God picked as Israel's next king. Yet here he stood, back in the same meadow, tending his father's sheep, with the sun going down behind his back and a gentle breeze cooling the sweat on his brow.*

It would appear that nothing had really changed in his life, and yet David knew in his heart that everything had changed. From one sunrise to the next, his destiny had been forever altered. He couldn't even begin to imagine all his Lord had in store for him.

Would he fight great battles? Would he defend Israel from her foes? Would he marry and have many children and produce a whole line of kings for their nation? Would he have good friends, someone to share in this strangely wonderful journey that he had just begun? So many questions drifted through his mind.

But there was one thing he was quite certain of, in his mind, his heart, and his soul: as the oil had poured down David's head, the Spirit of the Lord came upon him and gave him great power. He knew that he was set apart, chosen by God for great things, things he couldn't even dream of.

As the sun went down behind the rolling shoulders of the horizon, the sky burned pink and orange, tinted with blue, like a flame. He had never felt such joy, and his heart overflowed with words of thanksgiving and praise. He knelt in the tall grass and prayed out loud, saying words that would echo for eternity.

* * *

WHILE DAVID HAD BEEN ANOINTED AS KING BY GOD'S representative, notice that he did not immediately receive his crown and start ruling. That would all come later. In the meantime, what did David do? Rather than allowing the new revelation of his identity to inflate his ego, David humbly returned to the fields that he had come to know and love so well.

He displayed no entitlement, no sense of "I'm going to be king—there's no way I'm going back out and tend a bunch of smelly sheep!" He simply enacted a concept that is rare today: patient submission. At that point of his life, David was still his father's son and still bound to his father's assignment. He was a boy who would be king. But today he was still a herder of sheep, even though eventually he would be a ruler of men. He rested contentedly, knowing that the God who had sent for him once would send for him again at the next appointed time.

Just as we saw with Joseph, David's gift made room for him. It was time for the fruit of his secluded life in the wilderness to be exhibited before the whole world. The mark of favor on David's life took him from a private place of praise to a public platform of power.

The hand of the Lord was clearly upon the young shepherd's heart throughout the rest of his life's journey. Wherever David went, God went with him. The mark on his life granted his entrance into the royal palace, first as a musician and worshipper sent to soothe the ailing Saul, and then as its occupant, the king. God's favor continued to advance David from one level to the next, until he was eventually crowned king in the fulfillment of the anointing he had received years before.

David is one of my all-time favorite people in the Bible. He's larger than life, and bigger than his mistakes. He knew rejection, abandonment, loneliness, and obscurity firsthand, but he also experienced the favor and faithfulness of God. His life is another striking illustration of the seasons of destiny and the importance of divine timing.

How has God revealed your anointing to you? Where is he calling you to next? Do you have what it takes to be anointed in one area but temporarily assigned to another? Fulfilling our divine destiny requires patience, something that's often challenging in our world of instant gratification and 4G technology. We want to arrive at our final destination before we're barely out of the gate.

God's purposeful timing differs from our sense of possibility and probability. We look at externals, but God looks at our hearts. See, God knows when you're ready for what he's been *preparing you for* your entire life. David didn't know he had the future king of Israel inside him, and maybe he didn't even realize exactly what this meant after Samuel anointed him. But God knew it was there all along because that's who he created David to be.

Similarly, God knows what's inside of you that he has already anointed to come forth. He has selected you for something that no one else in this world can do but you. If you will accept his gift, and never forget the anointing that he's placed on you, then you will discover his abundance in every area of your life. Just because you're still out in the field, never doubt that someday you will be in the forefront!

CHAPTER TEN

Hope for the Hungry Heart

Do you have a favorite season of the year? A time when you feel totally alive and grateful for all that the season brings—particular kinds of weather, special foods, and holiday traditions? I know I do.

While a lot of people love spring and summer because they can be outside, I've never been an outdoorsy type of person. As a matter of fact, I think I'm allergic to the sun! Too much of it makes my head hurt, leaving me unable to open my eyes, let alone focus on the trees or flowers or whatever I'm supposed to be enjoying. Maybe that's why the Texas summers seem to leave me so exhausted—everything really is bigger in Texas! The sun is brighter, the heat is hotter, and the humidity is higher!

So I'm always excited when the season shifts into fall. Gone are the dog days of summer. No more outrageous electric bills from running the air conditioning 24/7. Put away the sunscreen and insect repellant. Get ready to go back to school and into normal routines. Bring out the sweaters and jackets.

There's just something special about fall. I love watching the leaves change color and feeling the brisk wind blow through my hair and across my face. The air is cooler and smells sweeter, ripe with the scent of apples.

And beyond my personal weather preferences, I like autumn because it seems to bring a shift not only inside me but in the minds of other people as well. Something about this particular season causes us to become more aware of the needs of others. Something about this particular season causes us to reflect on how good God has been to get us to where we are now.

Regardless of the time of year, our hearts are hungry for hope and we need to be reminded of all that the Lord provides for us. When our perspective changes, it somehow unlocks the grace that we need to get around every hurdle that threatens our progress. A shift in perspective can cause us to see that tough times are really just training times, and if we'll hang in there until God brings us out, we'll be much stronger than we were going in.

When I think about the many inspiring examples we see in the Bible, one stands out to me for the way he learned to keep his hope alive in the midst of some of the harshest of conditions. Elijah experienced super highs and super lows and had to have wondered what was going on. He knew God had called him to fulfill his purpose, yet nothing in his life ever seemed to get any easier.

THE MEMORY OF HIS CONFRONTATION WITH THE KING lingered in his mind. Elijah had heard so much about the deadly exploits of wicked King Ahab and his wife, Queen Jezebel, that he knew he was risking his life by appearing before the royal court. They were well known for pursuing and killing God's prophets. But Elijah also knew that God would protect him, even as he was in a battle not just with people's allegiance to pagan gods but also with the darkness of the human heart.

And now God had led him to Cherith, to a secluded wood near the rushing waters of a crystal brook. A grove of ficus trees and sycamore provided a natural shelter for him, offering shade from the scorching rays of the sun and a comfortable place to rest during the night. Apparently this was to be his campsite until the Lord told him otherwise.

Suddenly he heard flapping and, looking up, watched as a dark pair of wings soared toward him. As a raven landed on his out-stretched arm, Elijah marveled at this most unique messenger the Lord had sent to bring him food. (1 Kings 17)

LIKE ELIJAH, I'M ALWAYS AMAZED AT THE WAY GOD RE-veals his provision and his purposes. I know from firsthand experience that many of the times I have pressed and prayed through, even regarded as painful, were really just seasons in which God was preparing me for his purpose. I can't tell you how many times I thought dark times came because the devil was weakening me, only to look back and realize it was really God strengthening me! He was toughening me up, stretching me, teaching me that I could bear more than I ever thought possible. And in hindsight I can see now that it was all being done in a controlled environment—God's control.

I remember one afternoon as I was driving into my neighborhood, I saw a fire burning in the distance. As I got closer, I realized the flames came from a house that was al-ready surrounded by fire trucks, ambulances, and other emergency vehicles. Just before I panicked, my eyes caught a glimpse of a sign: TRAINING IN PROGRESS. I let out a deep sigh of relief. It was good to know that things were not as they first appeared. Whether it looked like it or not, everything was under control.

Now, I'll be honest with you: in my walk with the Lord I have found myself in places of panic. Had I seen the warning signs saying TRAINING IN PROGRESS, had I known that I was in a controlled environment, maybe I wouldn't have fought so hard to get out. Not that it did me any good anyway, because come what may, God had marked that place as a place of re-positioning in my life. I couldn't pray my way out of it, I couldn't confess, neither could I believe my way out! This was where God had me, and until further notice, I needed to "be still and know" (Ps. 46:10).

And what did I need to know? I needed to know that "he who started the work in my life would be faithful to complete it" (Phil. 1:6). To know that everything I had come through, come over, survived, outlasted, and outlived was God preparing me for what he was getting ready to do in my life.

Let me encourage you: everything that makes you press forward, makes you stretch, makes you cry, and makes you reach is for a reason! Everything you endure, encounter, and conquer—even those things you feel are conquering you right now—is for a reason. God wastes nothing in our lives and is always redeeming even the most painful of situations.

As a matter of fact, every place where you have experienced resistance in your life will ultimately make you stronger!

Where do you see yourself right now? Are you in a "training in progress" season, or is it still hard to understand what you're supposed to be "training" for? What are the biggest challenges blocking your path? In which areas of your life has God asked you to wait it out, trusting that he will move and let you know the next steps when the time is right? Have you seen any ravens overhead yet, bringing you nourishment while you wait?

His stomach rumbled like thunder and his throat was as dry as the desert. Day after day the sun beat down upon the parched land. How many weeks had it been, how many months into years? He had lost count. At first Elijah had noticed only subtle changes in the land. The grasses faded from emerald green to the color of pale palm branches. Now they were brown, as dry as tinder.

He was so hungry, and his hope seemed to be sinking faster than the water in the Cherith Brook. The banks alongside it had become muddy jaws slowly closing as the stream dwindled to a mere trickle.

Today he went to sip from the shallow puddles of remaining water—and there were none. The brook was completely dry and

only soft, moist earth remained. Had the Lord brought him here to
die of thirst? What was he supposed to do now?

DO ELIJAH'S QUESTIONS SOUND FAMILIAR? HAVE YOU
found yourself doing what the Lord told you to do only to
find it much more challenging than you expected? Moving into the fullness of your destiny is rarely a smooth, easy
process. It takes a certain measure of power to possess your
promises. There has to be something in you that refuses to
fall short of anything that God has given you permission to
have or to do. It takes real strength, and you should not be
shocked to discover that real strength comes through resistance. It is *pushing back* and not *caving in* that builds up stamina. Being successful is not cheap; there is always a cost factor
to consider. Expect to be inconvenienced. Expect to suffer!
Why? Because the Bible tells us that it's only after we've suffered a while that God will establish us and make us perfect (1
Pet. 5:10). *Not* suffering means *not* succeeding.

Some people might disagree with this statement because
they believe that suffering comes from disobedience to God.
But the Bible says, "All that will live godly in Christ Jesus
shall suffer persecution" (2 Tim. 3:12). This tells me that we
must understand that suffering for Christ and with Christ is
not optional. We're told, "And if [we are] children, then [we

are] heirs; heirs of God, and joint-heirs with Christ; if so be that we suffer with him, that we may be also glorified together" (Rom. 8:17). Suffering has been, and always will be, a part of the process of greatness! If we don't say yes to the process, we disqualify ourselves from the prize.

Believe me, I know firsthand how hard it is to see the hand of the Lord when everything seems to go from bad to worse. Growing up, I often heard my mother say that I was the child they hadn't planned on having. Not that I was unwanted, but I was certainly unexpected. When she found out she was having me, she cried. But what Momma didn't know was that two years after I was born, my sixteen-year-old sister was going to go home to be with the Lord. So my presence became a comfort.

Nevertheless, I was special from the beginning because I was the baby. I wasn't an only child (one of five), but I was very lonely growing up because my sisters were grown and married with families. So I grew up learning how to cope with loneliness, and because I didn't have siblings to play with, I formed a tight bond with my father, especially after he lost my sister Brenda.

My father told me that I was a princess. He made sure I knew that I was somebody. We lived in a small house in southwest Detroit. We didn't have a lot of money, but we didn't miss it because we had parents who loved us and raised us in the admonition of the Lord. Even today I consider myself to have had a rich childhood because while I may not have had things of monetary value, I had a father who told me who I was, and through his love he taught me I was priceless!

Just days before I turned twelve, my father died of a massive heart attack. A few months after he passed away, my mother was injured in a major car accident. Since it would take weeks, if not months, for her to recover, she moved in with one of my sisters while I stayed with a family from our church who lived close to my school. So now not only was I a lonely child, but I was also a grieving child because the losses were so overwhelming.

Within a year, my entire family structure had exploded and I found myself living with people that I loved, but as we all know, there is no place like home, and for me, no family like mine. I'm not sure I've ever been as frightened, lonely, grief stricken, and anxious as I was during that season. I felt like my childhood had been victimized overnight. However, as I look back, I realize that my childhood was not about my being a victim; it was about God teaching me how to be a leader.

Sometimes you don't know how important God is until he's all you've got, and it was during this lonely stage of my life that I began to build a relationship with him. He knew the plans for my life and began forming me to fit into the spot he had fashioned for me. He knew the personality I

would need. He knew the experiences I would have to endure. He had the blueprint for all that Sheryl was to become.
The loneliness, the grief, the displacement would all work
together for good.

Everything I went through, I shared with him. He walked
every step with me. He became not only my God, but my
friend, too. We went together like peanut butter and jelly. So
when I went through seasons in my life when friends would
walk away, I was like, "Okay, whatever," because I knew how
to be happy by myself. I knew how to play alone. I knew how
to get myself up and get dressed for school alone. I knew
how to spend hours and hours by myself.

And there was purpose in all of that. God knew how he
was going to use me. He knew that he was going to anoint
and appoint me. He knew that at certain points in my life,
people were going to hate me because of the way he would
choose to bless me. He also knew that when people hated me
I wouldn't flip out because he had already taught me how to
walk alone. As long as I had my friend Jesus, I was going to
be all right. As long as he was there, I knew that I was never
really alone.

I also learned at a very young age how to bury things and
people I really, really loved, and yet find a way to keep moving. You may know what I'm talking about. Whatever life has
handed you, you've learned how to play the hand you were
dealt. The enemy wants us to see ourselves as victims because

usually victims are powerless, and when you're powerless you feel as if everything is out of your control. Now granted, all of the changes I went through in my childhood were completely out of my control, but how I look back *now* over what I went through *then* is vital to my future. Often the difference between being *a victim* and *a victor* is perception, and the way I chose to get the last laugh was by refusing to allow my yesterday to dictate my today! By the grace of God, I learned how to be the type of person who could redefine "normal."

Now I see why God had to take me through all the grief and struggles; he knew I would one day become involved in ministry. He knew I'd become a singer, songwriter, and worship leader. He knew I would marry a preacher, become a preacher, host my own television show, pastor a church, travel the world as a conference speaker, and now author a book. He knew all that was ahead of me on my life's journey. He knew the twists and turns that I could never have imagined or anticipated. And he knew just what I needed to face them.

I encourage you to think back to some of the hardest seasons of your life and remember how God got you through them. It probably didn't happen the way you thought or hoped it would, but I'm guessing God got you through by making you stronger. He has surprised you in the past with moments that seemed much harder than you ever expected, and yet you've gotten to this moment in the present as a stronger, wiser, more mature believer.

DURING THE NIGHT, ELIJAH HAD HEARD THE VOICE OF *the Lord telling him where he must go, a place called Zarephath. As the city gate came within view, he saw an old woman gathering sticks in the ditches nearby. With his last ounce of strength, he surged toward her and said, "Would you please bring me some water? I've traveled so far and am so thirsty."*

She dropped her sticks in a heap and said, "Of course, sir. The well is up ahead—I'll be right back."

"Could you please bring me some bread, too?" he called out after her, panting.

She stopped immediately and turned around. "I'm sorry, but I do not have bread for you." She cast her eyes down at the ground as her voice grew softer. "I have only a pinch of flour and a few drops of oil. I've been gathering sticks for a fire so that I can bake bread for me and my son. It's all we have—after that, I'm afraid we will die."

"Do not worry," said Elijah to the widow. "You will have more than enough to eat. Go and build your fire and bake some bread. Bring it to me so that I may eat first. Then make more for you and your son. The Lord God of Israel says that your flour jar will never be empty, nor will your bottle of oil ever run dry. You will

have more than enough until God sends his rain over all the land."

Less than an hour later, she handed the grizzled prophet some bread on a palm leaf and placed a full water jug beside him. As she returned to her house and to the cooking corner next to the fire, she couldn't bear to look inside the clay jar from which she had just emptied the last of the flour. Surely she would have seen if there had been more in there. And the oil—she knew she had drained the final precious drops.

Then her eyes opened as wide as the morning sky! There was plenty of flour in her bin. And the bottle of oil appeared to be almost full! How could this have happened?

ARE YOU ONE OF THOSE PEOPLE WHO ALWAYS HAS A backup plan, a Plan B in case the most direct route doesn't take you where you need to go? Or are you more the type to get by on a wing and a prayer?

Sometimes following the Lord can feel like a scavenger hunt. We get to one place and then discover that it leads us to the next. We get there and find out that it's leading us in a different direction altogether. With each step, we start guessing what to anticipate and what he's up to. We trust him and figure we know what to expect. But often we're surprised, and in times like that, he allows us to discover deep within ourselves a strength that has been hidden in secret places.

One of the most life-altering moves my husband and I made was when we went to Nashville to plant a church. We had been doing itinerant ministry, and we were based in Detroit where my husband's father was pastoring a church. We were both very young and full of so much life! Things initially started out very well; however, as it turned out, Nashville would become a kind of Gethsemane for me. I moved there feeling as if we had everything. I went in with all kinds of hope, vision, and expectation. We were building a church and expecting it to be just wonderful. We had traveled to so many different places and seen so many successful churches that inspired us with ideas and concepts we were sure we could implement in Nashville.

I didn't preach at the time; I was the worship leader. One of my greatest joys was helping the people to prepare their hearts for the word of the Lord that my husband would so powerfully bring. I loved our church. I loved the people. The longer I was there, the more involved I became in their lives. It just felt right. I felt part of my purpose was to help them find their purpose in life.

I wore many hats in this ministry. I was the nanny/delivery service/secretary or whatever I was needed to be. I loved these people, and if they had a problem, I just wanted it fixed. If I could help them get where they were going by becoming a bridge, that's what I wanted to do. I had a lot of experience when it came to needing a bridge, now I was ready to be one!

One couple in our church was comprised of an African-American young man and his Caucasian wife. They had a baby girl named Sandi. Sandi's mother was in school, and her father was working, so Sandi needed a babysitter. This was a perfect situation to be used by the Lord, I thought, so I became Sandi's babysitter. It had been a while since my girls were small, but I learned that taking care of a baby is a lot like riding a bicycle: if you've done it once, you can do it again. It didn't take long for me to become attached to little Miss Sandi.

Wherever I went, Sandi went. She was my sidekick. She had an infectious smile, and I fell in love with her. I treated her as if she were my very own, never knowing that one day my grandbabies would be interracial. I had never been given the privilege to love an interracial child before. Why was that happening to me? Why did I look at her day after day, amazed at her beauty? Amazed at the beautiful color of her skin? No tanning bed, no spray tan, no weekend beach excursion would ever cause me to have a color as beautiful as hers naturally was. What was that about? You see, if you just look back over your life, the Lord will give you clues all along the way as to what he has planned for you.

There was another lady in our church who had a cooking

business. Just as Sandi's family had worked their way into my heart, she did, too. I wanted her to make it. She was a single mother. She was a great cook, but she didn't have a vehicle. So there I was, often with Sandi in tow, delivering plate lunches all over the city of Nashville in my old Volvo with a broken air conditioner and only one window that rolled down. Remembering times like those makes me want to praise God! However, don't let my praise confuse you, because while I don't want to ever go through them again, I wouldn't take anything for them.

I would be running all over Nashville, delivering these boxes filled with delicious-smelling lunches, many of them to the record companies all up and down Music Row. I was so happy going from one office to the next with these boxes because I knew that Sherry's business was doing so well! Little did I know that a few years later I would be writing songs those publishing companies would carry around the world. I didn't know it then, but God did! And while I was making it happen for Sherry, he was making it happen for me.

There's something about helping others that will cause God to help you, too. He'll work behind your back. He'll be pulling stuff together for your future, even while you're struggling in the middle of your today. And if your heart passes the test, he'll make you a blessing while you're being a blessing.

In Nashville, we had another faithful member in our

church named Ellis who owned a tour bus company. One day I learned that some things were going a little crazy in his business and he needed office help. Ellis told me that his secretary had quit to pursue another career. Her name was Faith Hill, and I'm guessing you can tell what happened with her—she left to sing her way into stardom. Because Ellis was so faithful to our vision, I decided the least I could do was to be faithful to his until he found someone better to help him. I loved him and I wanted him to make it!

Yet with hindsight I can see it was more than that. This was once again God leaving me with yet another clue. Little did I know, a few years later my family and I would be traveling the roads for Jesus in one of those tour buses, and guess who would be behind the wheel? Ellis! The man that I was working for then was *now* working for me!

Looking back over my life as Sandi's day-care provider, Sherry's lunch plate deliverer, and Ellis's secretary, I realize that this had all been orchestrated by someone bigger than me. This was the Lord's doing. I just wanted that church to grow and I wanted God to bless it.

We had no financial base outside of what we brought in strictly through tithes and offerings. Because of this, we were always challenged with financial issues. Many times we had to choose between buying groceries and buying gas to get us back and forth to the services. Times were very hard for us. We pawned everything valuable we had to keep the lights on, the doors open, and food on our table. We were in some of the darkest nights and tightest places we had ever experienced.

All I could do was hope and pray that this season of our lives had an expiration date attached to it. It took all the faith I had each day to get out of bed and show up for the fight. "What fight?" you might ask. The fight to survive! I would often go to my Bible and read the words of the apostle Paul: "There hath no temptation taken you such as is common to man: but God is faithful, who will not suffer you to be tempted above that ye are able; but will with the temptation also, make a way to escape, that ye may be able to bear it" (1 Cor. 10:13).

I've heard preachers quote this verse for years. Most of the time they were referring to temptation as something strictly related to sin and lust. Yet these are not the only temptations we face in life. What about the temptation to quit? To walk away? To lose the faith and throw in the towel? What about the temptation to give yourself the permission to wave your flag of surrender as you are crumbling under the weight of life? I was *there*!

I was borrowing from Peter to pay Paul. Pouring water in the milk to stretch it. Swimming upstream, trying to hold it all together. Smiling on the outside, but dying on the inside. Preaching faith yet living in fear. Laying hands on the sick yet going home sick myself. Trying to juggle the things I could see, all the while bracing for the things I couldn't see.

Trying to navigate and work my way through the land mines of my life. Things that came out of nowhere. Things that knocked the breath out of me. Burdens that blindsided me. Contrary winds that blew in bills, betrayals, and broken dreams in the middle of the night.

My home, my family, my mind, my marriage, my ministry—everything about me was hurting and I wanted to quit! I wanted to give up and become a victim of my circumstances! If it shocks you to hear me say this, I am sorry. I know it doesn't sound very spiritual, but it is very human. And I don't care how spiritual we are, we all have human reactions to life!

I didn't know it then, but what I was feeling wasn't that unusual. What I was feeling was "common to man." No matter what your name is, who you know, or who you are, life can sometimes slap you so hard that you just want to quit! My husband and I kept thinking that the tide was about to turn, that things were going to get better, that soon we could see the light at the end of the tunnel—all because we knew we were where God wanted us to be. And we did everything we could to make the most of a trying situation. In hindsight, it's almost comical how many things went so wrong, one after another.

But often these are the most crucial times for us to let go of our expectations. If we ever want to discover the greatness that God has planted inside us, then we have to be willing to rely on him unconditionally—and not just when it feels good or when we're so desperate that there's no other option. God wants our attention focused on him so that we'll go wherever he leads us without talking back.

In the midst of those moments, it usually feels like the hardest thing we've ever done. But greatness always requires sacrifice to activate it. We should take comfort in realizing that what we sacrifice now is nothing compared to what we're about to gain. God has more for us than we can imagine, and if we cling to the past we won't be able to embrace his new gifts. In order to receive all God has for us, sometimes the best plan is just to put our faith in action.

The reality is that no matter how many plans we make, God holds the master plan that trumps them all! Sometimes we try to control our lives so much that we forget to leave room for God to work. It's good to have a plan, and good to have a Plan B up our sleeves in case our first one fails, but eventually the only plan that matters is *Plan G*! When we follow God, we must be prepared to move quickly, to change course when he tells us, and to let go of our limited, human expectations.

After about a year and a half into this ministry we had birthed, we began to realize it wasn't going to make it. It was like carrying a child for nine months, preparing for its arrival, setting up the nursery, buying all the little clothes, blankets, and diapers, giving birth to it, and after all of that, it dies in your arms, under your watchful eye, while being cradled in your tender care. I asked God, "Why? Why did you let me have it if you knew it wasn't going to live? What was the point? What was the purpose? Why did you let me love it? Why the birth pains? Why did it die? How do you expect me to keep on living?"

He awoke from his nap, startled at the commotion. The widow was beating her hands against Elijah's chest, her tears flying like the raindrops they had not seen in years. "It's your fault!" she wailed. "My son is dead and it's because of you! Is it not enough that you come and make me aware of all the ways I fall short of the holiness of the Lord? Must you take the only one I love away from me now? You are a heartless man and you serve a cruel God!"

He tried to comfort her, but she would not have it. She buried her face in her hands. He didn't understand what had happened before his very eyes, the boy's health waning away. He kept thinking that the boy would get better—and now this. Surely his death could not be what the Lord intended!

"Bring him to me—I will take care of this," he said. The woman then brought the boy to Elijah, who took him to his sleeping chamber and ministered to him there. The child's body was as pale as a lily and as cool as the shade of a sycamore. He was not breathing. Elijah hovered over the lifeless body and pleaded with God to breathe new life into the child. He knew God could do this and begged him to do it now. "Do not abandon these people who have

been faithful to your purposes! Show them that you are a God of life, a God of joy, a God who loves them!"

After he had prayed the third time, after he had lain over the boy's crumpled body, Elijah felt something move ever so slightly beneath him. Then he felt the boy's breath on his cheek! God had given new life to this child; he had answered Elijah's prayers. The boy sat up then, as if waking from a dream, and smiled. The prophet took him by the hand and led him into the other room, where his mother was still crying.

"What's wrong, Momma?" he asked. "Don't worry—I feel much better now."

His mother shrieked with disbelief and threw her hands around her son's shoulders. In a matter of moments, her tears of sorrow had been transformed into a fountain of joy.

HAVE YOU EVER LOST SOMETHING PRECIOUS TO YOU AND then had it restored? Maybe it was your marriage or your health. It could be your career, your reputation, or your church family. You thought the life had been taken from it, and you began grieving. And then, in the middle of your grief, God brought it back to you, more full of life and breath than it was before.

Elijah and the widow of Zarephath knew what that was like. They had already sacrificed so much to get to where they were. The widow had given her food and her trust to this man of God. She was barely scraping by as it was, but then to lose something so precious as the life of a child must have seemed unbearable. But through Elijah's faith and God's power, through the love of a mother for her son, the little boy started to breathe again, his lungs filled with air, and his heart began to beat.

God wants to resurrect our dreams, even the ones we thought we lost a long time ago, if we'll let him. Sometimes you have to lose something before you realize how much you have or how much you appreciate it. Sometimes you have to lose a job to appreciate a paycheck. Sometimes you have to lose a relationship to appreciate a real friend.

When God breathes new life into your heart, you discover the grace to handle things you could not handle before. And once you've adjusted your perspective, you no longer see your situation as a place of trouble but as a place of training. Once your perspective changes, you know you're not going to be taken out of the fight, only toughened up for the next one. You can tell the devil, "If you think I'm going to quit after this, forget it! It's going to take more than this to stop me! I've been through enough in my life to know God is faithful. And I've learned how to adjust my perspective and see that he's good all the time."

* * *

THE CAVE WAS SO DARK THAT ELIJAH COULD NOT SEE HIS hand in front of him. He was scared this time, afraid that his life was finally over. Enamored with pagan gods from foreign lands, Ahab and Jezebel were in hot pursuit, and the evil woman had made it clear that she would not rest until Elijah was dead. He had fled into the wilderness, with her soldiers in hot pursuit.

Finally, he could go no farther and collapsed, panting, beneath a broom bush. "I'm through, Lord. Take my life and let me join my ancestors." He fell asleep, exhausted.

An angel had awakened him then and told him to nourish himself. He was amazed to see a small fire, where hot bread and a jar of cool water waited for him. He ate and slept again. When he woke next, the angel told him to eat and drink some more, that the journey was still too much with him.

Strengthened by the nourishment the Lord provided, Elijah then traveled forty days and nights to Horeb, the mountain of God, where he slept on the cold dirt floor of a small cave. Suddenly, he heard the voice of the Lord asking him, "What are you doing here, Elijah?"

Elijah answered the Lord, who then instructed him to go to a mountaintop where he would reveal himself. The climb was perilous, and along the way, Elijah witnessed earthquakes, rock slides, and firestorms, but none contained the voice of God with further instruction. Finally, the wind shifted and a gentle breeze began to blow. The voice of the Lord whispered in his ear. (1Kings 19:1–15)

* * *

WHEN MY HUSBAND AND I WERE WORKING SO HARD TO make our lives and ministry work in Nashville, I remember someone asking, "What are you going to do if this doesn't work out?" I said, "Doesn't work out? It *has* to work out! We're here for the duration. We'll be here the rest of our lives as far as we know." We were going for broke, and broke is exactly what we got.

Our bank account was broken. Our confidence was broken. Our spirits were broken. Our pride was broken. Our vision was broken. My heart was broken. My body was broken, and I couldn't even afford to go anywhere to get it fixed. I didn't know what was going on anymore. We were doing everything we knew to do. I mean, if we had known a better way we would've done it.

I don't have any real answers as to why the church dwindled and died except perhaps God allowed it to dry up like Elijah's brook, forcing us to move on to the next assignment he had planned for us. Nashville became a grain of wheat that fell to the ground and died, thus becoming the seed that produced the harvest that I am bringing in today.

Finally, we began to move through our struggles and realize that we were passing through a training season. At the time I told God, "You brought us here to build a successful church." Later I realized he was saying, "No, I brought you here to build a successful leader." He was teaching me through all those experiences how to be—and how not to be—a pastor. Ironically, he was teaching me how to lead in a place where I would never be given an opportunity to lead.

I thought my painful position would destroy me, but it was really just a place for my personal preparation. I cried there, but it wasn't for there. It was never meant to work there because it was simply a training ground. I fasted there, but it wasn't for there. I served there, but it wasn't for there. I prayed there, but it wasn't for there. And no matter how much I tried to get it to work, it would not work there. My husband and I used every ounce of faith we had to make it work, but it clearly wasn't destined to be.

Finally, we knew it was time to leave. There was no sign of life. It was over. It was time to pronounce the benediction on that season in my life so I could move on. I walked away from Nashville just as you would walk away from a gravesite. The entire church moved on. Ellis was the last member standing, and we embraced him like family and are still very close to him.

I thought I was through with ministry. I wanted nothing else to do with it. I loved God, but I was just going to be a good member at someone else's church. For the longest time I wouldn't even talk about it. I was numb. I felt like a failure. We couldn't even talk about it between ourselves. Sometimes you don't realize how hard you've pushed until it's over.

I didn't understand it until God came to me and said, "Sheryl, you have to forgive the process." Never once did I believe I had to forgive God. He does all things well. However, the pain that I went through, the depression, the regret, the mistakes that caused me to make choices that left me feeling like a failure: those things were all wrapped up in the word *process*. I needed to be able to say, "You lied to me, but it's okay. You left the church, but it's okay. You weren't there for me when I needed you most, but I forgive you."

Forgiving the process is a very important step because when we forgive these types of things, God then in turn works it all together for our good. He reveals, "I was just getting you ready for where I needed to take you eventually." I couldn't see where all the pain would lead, but he could. I didn't think I had the strength to endure, but God knew it was there. He knew what was inside me and was cultivating it for when it would be needed most. The whole process and experience were preparation for a future role.

There is a promise over our lives that God wants to bring to pass, but he often has to take us through a repositioning phase first. And it's confusing and heart wrenching because you know you're following him and his will for your life, but your expectations have been dashed on the rocks of hard times.

This is when you must keep going, step by step, day by day. This is when your hungry heart must follow the daily bread crumbs God always gives and accept that you have enough hope for today. These morsels take many forms,

from a sense of God's presence during the day to an unexpected kindness from a complete stranger. You recognize
them by paying attention and asking God to show you.

You may not have enough for tomorrow or ten years
from now, but you have enough for today. Eventually you
can thank God for giving you the grace to come through the
fire without being burned. Your clothes may smell like smoke
for a while, and you may feel a little hot under the collar, but
you survived.

The Bible says, "O give thanks unto the Lord, for He is
good" (Ps. 107:1). Sometimes you have to walk with him for
a while to realize just how good he is. Sometimes you have to
let some time go by before you can see his purpose in a painful situation. And then nobody has to tell you to give him
thanks. It's just natural because you know what he has done
in your life.

Giving thanks to the Lord for all he's brought you
through is a wonderful thing. I often find myself simply saying "Thank you, Lord." In spite of all the poetic words, and
all the beautiful songs we've been given, in spite of all of the
artists who have created so many wonderful ways to worship
God, sometimes there's nothing to do but say simply, "Thank
you. Thank you, Jesus."

The Bible says that from the rising of the sun to the
going down of the same, the name of the Lord is to be
praised (Ps. 113:3). He is mighty, he is great, and he is greatly

to be praised. I encourage you to thank him for all the "training sessions" you've endured and all the lessons learned. Thank him for the hard ways that the treasure inside you has been uncovered so that you are now fulfilling your divine destiny, becoming all you were meant to be. Thank him for knowing what you needed even when you didn't know it yourself!

If you're in the midst of a "training session" right now, be encouraged that this season will not destroy you. It will prepare you. As painful as all the blows may feel, cling to God and trust him to bring you through it. Praise him for where he's leading you and how well equipped you'll be once you arrive.

The Ultimate Treasure

Have you ever watched one of those TV shows where people take their antiques (and even sometimes their junk!) from the attic and have it appraised by an expert? It's always amazing to see someone take a little vase they got from their great-grandmother and discover that it once belonged to royalty and is now worth thousands of dollars. Or that old wooden chair with the wobbly arm? Handmade by a famous carpenter and worth a hundred times what you paid for it at a yard sale! That pretty oil painting of roses? Worth more than your house!

Those shows are fun because they remind us that something may appear ordinary, but in fact it is actually quite rare and valued so much more highly than we ever dreamed. Similarly, I believe we often have to be reminded of the priceless treasure God has placed inside each of us. Maybe we've caught glimpses of our future or been anointed by him to move into a certain role, but through the day-in, day-out drudgery of life we forget who we are and where we're going.

As we've explored each of these ten heroes of the faith, I hope you've been reminded not to give up your dream or to despair in dire conditions. You may find yourself like Ruth and Naomi, trying to start over again in uncertain times. Maybe you're looking for a new job or you've literally had to move to another city. Maybe your move is only internal, a shifting of your heart from the losses of the past to the abundance of the future.

Maybe you feel as if it's too late for God to use you because of all the mistakes and selfish choices you've made. Rahab reminds us that there's truly treasure in each one of us that God calls forth to accomplish his purposes. All we have to do is trust him and grab the lifeline he extends to us. It's never too late.

You may find yourself wanting to see your dream come

to life, and you just can't stop thinking about your heart's desire. Hannah reminds us that as long as we remember that we are stewards of his gifts and not entitled owners, he will be faithful to bring new life into our dreams. Others may even think we're drunk or flat-out crazy, but we know that persistence pays off when we're following God.

Or maybe you find yourself at a crossroads with God, wondering if you really know who you are and where you're going. Like Jacob, you're in a wrestling match, pushing and pulling with the circumstances of your life even as you beg for God's blessing. In these struggles, you must always remember that God knows you better than you know yourself, that he calls you by your true name, and he will deliver on all he promises, even when we try to accelerate the process or get in his way.

Your new identity might be one you could never have imagined for yourself. Just as God chose a timid man like Gideon to be his mighty warrior, we are often called to become so much more than the roles we've played thus far. We can question God's selection, set fleeces for confirmation, and doubt that we've heard correctly. But if we're walking with the Lord, we have to be prepared to step into the spotlight when it's our time.

Noah certainly did. When he was singled out by God for his righteousness while everyone around him turned away, Noah and his wife discovered that their trust in God allowed them to create something the world had never seen and to preserve a legacy that we still celebrate to this day. No matter how inconsequential or insignificant we may feel we are, everything we do matters.

Just ask Naaman and his maid: they know how a small hinge can swing a mighty door. Because this young woman refused to become a victim to her circumstances, she saved the life of her master and reflected the life-giving glory of God to everyone around her.

Certainly it's not always easy to keep the faith in the midst of feeling broken, battered, and betrayed. Joseph experienced blows that he never saw coming—at the hands of his family, no less. But he remained faithful throughout his ordeals because he was ordained. He knew that God never abandoned him. And he lived to see God use him in miraculous ways to preserve the lives of millions of people. He knew that forgiveness was an essential part of fulfilling his God-given destiny.

Patience is also an important part of our faith journey, and a shepherd boy named David became living proof. Anointed by the prophet Samuel to be God's king, David nonetheless returned to his father's fields and remained faithful in the small things until it was time to follow God to the forefront and do big things. He might not have looked like a king, but David discovered that God looks on the inside, not on outward appearances.

Finally, the prophet Elijah reminds us that even in the midst of following God and fulfilling our purpose we will still face unexpected challenges. Only when we rely on God for everything—*everything*—do we grow through the hard times and become the mature, beautiful, fulfilled children of God he created us to be. We must never lose faith, no matter how bleak things appear or what losses we sustain. God gives us back what we thought we had lost and fills our emptiness with an abundance of blessings we could never have imagined.

As we conclude our time together within these pages, I leave you with one last example of what it means to find the faith to finish well. In everything Jesus did here on earth, he honored his Father and reflected God's goodness. Whether he was turning water into wine, healing the diseased and disabled, or feeding people with the nourishment of his Word, Jesus displayed an intimate trust that gives us a model to follow as we discover the treasure that God has placed inside us.

Even as he sweated blood and asked God if there was some other way to accomplish his purposes, Jesus submitted himself to his Father. In the Garden of Gethsemane, he prayed, "Not my will, but thine" (Luke 22:42). He never lost faith even as he suffered unto death. In all the torturous pain on the cross, Jesus trusted that God would do what he said he would do. Jesus knew that he would return from the dead and bring new life to everyone throughout all time.

There's no way I could write only one chapter on the many examples of Christ's faithfulness, but I also could not bear to end this book without him. He knows what it means to find lasting fulfillment in accomplishing his Father's will. Jesus calls us forward and reminds us that no matter where we are, the journey isn't over.

The Bible says, "The Lord is good unto them that wait for Him" (Lam. 3:25) and "Blessed are all they that put their trust in Him" (Ps. 2:12). God has a plan of significance, purpose, and abundance for your life. You must hold on to faith to finish what he has started in you. You may feel like giving up on life, on yourself, on the church, on other people, and even on God, but he has never given up on you and he never will. No matter who you think you are or what you've done, he loves you, and seeing you prosper is at the top of his wish list. "Beloved, I wish above all things that thou mayest prosper" (3 John 1:2).

Believe him for the impossible, the unimaginable, the unobtainable. If he has called you to accomplish something, you can rely on it happening. Even when it doesn't happen according to your timetable, wait on him and do not grow faint. You are closer to your divine destiny than ever before. Don't give up a few minutes before the miracle! Don't let go of your grasp on greatness!

As we close out this book, I want to leave you with one of

my favorite Scriptures. Ephesians 1:9 says, "Having made known unto us the mystery of his will according to his good pleasure, which he hath purposed in himself." Notice it doesn't say having known the mystery of his will, but rather "having *made* known." That means there's a process to knowing this mysterious thing called the will of God. It means that, little by little, he lets us in on the plans he has already laid out for our lives. It doesn't happen all at once—it happens incrementally. It happens "Line upon line and precept upon precept" (Isaiah 28:10). It happens in moments of worship, for it is in worship that you come to know him. And knowing him is vital, because you can never know *you* until you first know *him*. If you don't know his will for your life, I challenge you to worship him, and as you tell him who he is, he will tell you who you are. If you don't know what is in you, I challenge you to keep searching. Gifts evolve over a lifetime, and if you're not through living, you shouldn't be through searching for the hidden treasure in your earthen vessel. Walk with confidence, because everything you will ever need is within you. Live your life to the fullest, because when you have the ultimate treasure, you really are the total package.

ACKNOWLEDGMENTS

Thank you to Dudley Delffs. Your insight, wisdom, and years of experience helped make this book a success. To Jan Miller and Shannon Marven at Dupree Miller and Associates, you have been with me every step of the way. Thank you for the many phone calls, emails, and meetings that occurred to bring this book fruition. You have truly helped make a dream come true for me. Thank you to the entire team at Howard Books and Simon & Schuster. Thank you to Jonathan Merkh for recognizing my potential as an author. I will always be grateful for the trust you have placed in me. Thank you to Becky Nesbitt for lending your expertise and thoughtfulness to the editing process.

To my SBM staff: To say you're the best is an understatement! The precious passion you pour out daily is priceless. Chris, Tina, Marc, Lana, Nina, Travis, Kay, Rose, Joseph, Tameka, Manny, and Zera, thank you for making it all happen even when it means leaving your lane, dropping your title, and becoming liquid. Thanks for extending my reach and touching God's people with genuine compassion!

Your gifting speaks volumes, but the simplicity of your heart resounds even louder!

To my Potter's House and River Church families: One of my greatest joys is to watch you discover the hidden treasure within your vessel. Thank you for continuing to pull your chair up to my table! My prayer is that the bread of heaven will feed you until you want no more.

Thanks to my ministry friends around the world who have opened their pulpits and their hearts to me. I am honored to call you my friends.

To my sisters Elaine and Kay, their husbands, and all of my nieces and nephews: We are the definition of a true family! We've been marked and chosen by God. Heaven hears us and hell knows us, because the devil's worst nightmare is a PRAYING FAMILY! From one generation to another, we will declare the mighty acts of God! "As for me and my house, we *will* serve the Lord!"

To Pastor Donald and Mary Lou Brady: Thank you for opening up and allowing me to be part of such a great family. From the very beginning I have felt your love and acceptance. I couldn't have asked for a greater father and mother-in-law. You are two of God's choicest vessels. You are Godly people to the core, and as your children, that has and always will leave a huge impact on our lives. I love you both with all my heart!

To my three sons: Marc, you are like the gift that keeps on giving. Is there *anything* that you can't do? Your capacity to *learn*, as well as *teach*, seems to be limitless! By the grace of God you have found a way to jump in and play so many of the roles that my life's drama has called for. Thank you for all the lives you've touched when no one was looking. Your life is making the difference for more people than you'll ever know. Never forget that "when you have done it unto the least of these, you have done it unto Him." Thank you for continually dreaming and finding ways to take me to the uttermost parts of the earth. Thank you for walking with me through the midnight hours with this book. Often it was your words of encouragement that gave me the grace to keep going. Thanks for not letting me quit.

Chris, I fell in love with you first because of the father I saw that you were to Harmony. You broke every preconceived idea I had of a single father. I watched you come off the road after traveling with me from church to church and city to city, only to jump in your car on very little sleep and drive hours roundtrip to pick Harmony up on a Saturday night so she could be in church with you on Sunday morning. And now to see you with Jaden and Josiah, cultivating their gifts and covering them with the same kind of fatherly love that I admired from a distance—it sure makes me one proud "GeGe"! You are the soundtrack to everything "ministry" in my life. When we tap into those "music from heaven moments," the miraculous happens! For years people have heard the great music you make, but I find it my honor to tell them that the man behind the music is even greater!

Travis, I'll never forget looking across the congregation one Sunday morning and seeing a young man worship like I had always imagined the Psalmist David would. Sunday after Sunday you caught my eye. I loved how you loved God unashamedly. When I looked at you, the Scripture that always came to mind was, "Oh that Men would praise the Lord." I was clueless that the man who worshipped God with total abandonment would one day become my son. However, you did, and over the years I've observed God as He has reached deep into your potential and pulled out amazing things. I've watched as He has taken you from a face in the crowd to a part of our praise team, to an armor bearer, to a Duke Divinity school graduate, to a youth pastor, and now the young adult pastor at The Potter's House! Keep worshiping, keep praying, and keep listening for His voice. He will talk you into everything He has called you to be. You are gifted with greatness and I'm privileged to be a coach in your ear!

To my daughters: Lana, you not only rock, you *are* a rock! You are as consistently solid as they come. You are Nana. You are everybody's mother around our house. You stabilize us, calm us, and faithfully remind us that family is what really matters. The price that you have paid privately so that we can do what we do publicly has been enormous. It would have bankrupted most. Yet your life is a timeless textbook on how to find your purpose while empowering others to *find* and *do* theirs. You are as anointed to do what you do on the home front as I am in the forefront. As a heads-up, let me warn you to get ready, get ready, get ready, because you won't stay behind the scenes forever. There are too many people who need to hear how you do what you do. I am so proud of you. We are stuck together for life. We are like peanut butter and jelly! We just go together, and we're good anytime, anyplace.

Nina, you are so discerning. Like a watchman on the wall,

you have stood guard, crying loud and sparing not against everything and everyone who might even remotely threaten who we are as a family. You have the eyes of an eagle, the roar of a lion, and the heart of a lamb. None of that is by accident. You are evolving into your life's purpose. Little by little, God is unwrapping the gifts that He hid in you before the foundations of the world. I wait with great expectation to see you in all of your fullness. I'll be your biggest fan, screaming with the loudest voice every step of the way! Just remember, no matter how big you become, you will always be my baby. You are a quiet storm that should never be underestimated.

Tina, my born leader! You came into the world announcing that you were at large and in charge! Your first sphere of influence was your sisters. Whatever you all were doing, I always knew you were the ringleader. You've always had the power of persuasion! On top of your leadership abilities, God has anointed you with courage, cleverness, consistency, ingenuity, and insight. I love your heart toward the people of God. I love the way that you will totally turn our SBM offices into a sanctuary in a New York minute, calling out the names of those who have reached out to us to stand in agreement with them in prayer. You amaze me as you boldly rip open the heavens, week after week, worshipping as a reliever for some and as a forerunner for others. You are my Ruth and I am your Naomi. You have tapped into my rhythm for a reason. The field you have so faithfully poured the prime of your life into will one day, very soon, be yours. Why? Because of the predestined plan of God laced with your diligence. Every ounce of water you have poured onto my hands will be recycled into your dreams, because God is not unjust and will not forget your labor of love.

To Bishop and First Lady Jakes: To get from Moab to Bethlehem, Ruth needed Naomi. To get from his father's field to the forefront of a nation, David needed a prophet by the name of Samuel and a friend named Jonathan. Just like every Joshua needs a Moses, every Elisha needs an Elijah, and every Timothy needs a Paul, to get from where I was twenty years ago to where I am today, I needed you. You have steadily given me a hand up. I understand why I would reach for yours, but I am still humbled that you would reach back for mine. Thank you for preaching to me. Every message empowered me a little more to *stop* being who I was, so I could *start* being who I am! Thank you for being my sponsor and speaking up for me, announcing to my next level that it was time to open up and let me in. Thank you for teaching me to have sense enough to know that I must never let a Moabite mentality smother and suffocate my Bethlehem opportunity! You both have sown more into my life than time permits me to tell. I am as determined as a daughter to make sure that "your latter house is greater than the former." Your vision is my mission and while others may love you louder, they will *never* love you more!

Mom: Thanks to the greatest mother in the world! You were my first introduction to Jesus. As a child, I saw Him in your eyes, and it made me want to know Him. Thank you for always keeping me safe and secure. Still to this very day, one of my favorite hiding places is in your arms. Everything I am is a direct result of you! Your fingerprints are all over my life.

Your voice is on repeat in my soul. I may use *my* microphone, but I am preaching *your* message. I will always cherish you and work diligently to secure you. I wish everyone could know you. Those who haven't had that privilege will miss out on an opportunity to be touched by a real-life angel, because just like your name, that's exactly what you are!

To my amazing husband: If a picture paints a thousand words, then the smile on my face when I think of you should tell it all. Thank you for strongly supporting me over the years while God continued to wake up the sleeping things inside of me. Thank you for your leadership, your covering, your blessing, your faith, your wisdom, and your very precise perception. Your capacity to encourage me and countless others in the pursuit of purpose is unparalleled. Your car is the *baddest* phone booth on wheels. It's where you turn into Superman and solve the problems of preachers around the world! I love your heart for leaders. Whether they are young or old, rich or poor, famous or not so famous, whether they lead a congregation of two or 20,000, you find time to help each and every one of them. You are a preacher's friend, but at the end of the day, you are MINE! I am a better person because of you. Your presence gives me confidence. Your tender touch gently reminds me that whatever I am in, I am *not* in it alone! Thank you for the gift of our children. You have been a real father and a wonderful husband. We have been holding hands now for thirty-five years, and I'm asking God to give me at least one thousand more.